Constitutions, Taxation, and Land Policy: Volume II

Discussion and Analysis of Federal and State Constitutional Constraints on the Use of Taxation as an Instrument of Land-Planning Policy

Michael M. Bernard
Lincoln Institute of Land Policy

LexingtonBooks
D.C. Heath and Company
Lexington, Massachusetts
Toronto

For Daphne
Who exceeded Apollo
Through change and growth

Library of Congress Cataloging in Publication Data

Bernard, Michael M
    Constitutions, taxation, and land policy.

    Vol. 2 has title: Discussion and analysis of Federal and State constitutional
constraints on the use of taxation as an instrument of land-planning policy.
    Bibliography: v. 2, p.
    1. Real property and taxation—United States. 2. Land use—Law and
legislation—United States. 3. United States—Constitutional law. I. Title.
KF6535.B47   343'.73'054   78-24792
ISBN 0-669-02823-1 (vol. 1)
ISBN 0-669-03462-2 (vol. 2)

Published simultaneously in Canada

Printed in the United States of America

International Standard Book Number: 0-669-03462-2

Library of Congress Catalog Card Number: 78-24792

Contents

List of Tables

Preface

This is the second volume to appear under the general title of *Constitutions, Taxation, and Land Policy*. The first work, published by Lexington Books in 1979, contained the subtitle *Abstracts of Federal and State Constitutional Constraints on the Power of Taxation Relating to Land-Planning Policy*. During that year, in the aftermath of California's "Proposition 13," a great deal of interest had been generated in the areas of property taxation, constitutional tax limitation, and tax reform in general. This activity immediately revealed the pressing need for a current, convenient reference source that would afford easy access to the pertinent constitutional limitations or constraints on the taxing power and would be useful for informational as well as comparative-law purposes.

It may therefore be said that the order of publication of our research was somewhat reversed, so as to meet the pressing need, and we may now enter into our original exploration of the subject of land and regulatory taxation and its regulatory limits. In pursuing the analysis, reference to the first volume should prove particularly helpful and time saving, which is certainly its intended purpose.

Two basic subjects will be approached here. The first is how regulatory taxation has fared in the U.S. Supreme Court (chapters 4 and 5); the second is the nature of the state constitutional constraints as they have developed in the fifty states and the Commonwealth of Puerto Rico (chapter 6). The theoretical sources and nature of the taxing power at both the state and federal levels of government will also be discussed (chapters 2 and 3).

In pursuing the analysis, some 270 U.S. Supreme Court cases, as well as cases from other courts, have been reviewed in connection with the federal constitutional constraints on the regulatory taxing powers of the states and on the regulatory taxing power of the federal government itself. An alphabetized table of these cases will be found at the end of this volume. Following that, a table of citations to the applicable provisions of the U.S. Constitution has also been included.

With regard to state (and commonwealth) constitutions, the attempt here has been mainly to identify and categorize the pertinent clusters of constraints as they have appeared in the constitutions of the fifty-one cited jurisdictions. These were found to lend themselves best to tabular citation at this particular stage of the study. A list of the twenty-three tables that have been developed for the major categories will be found immediately following the table of contents at the beginning of this volume.

Finally, a list of selected cited references, including law review articles, is included. It should be understood that a far more extensive bibliography on the larger subject is under preparation as part of the study. At the end of this book, an addendum to the first volume has also been included to assure a maximum coverage of the abstracted textual material in conjunction with the tabular citations found herein.

It is hoped that the publication of this research work at the Lincoln Institute will help to provide the public and its officials, as well as the professional community, with some assistance in dealing with the very difficult problems of tax reform and the development of effective land planning policies.

Introduction from the
First Volume

Scope of the Larger Research Study

We are all familiar with the revenue-raising functions of taxation, yet there is another very important aspect that has always accompanied the basic effort to raise money for the operation of government: the potentially powerful *regulatory* effect of taxing measures. Perhaps in no instance is this more dramatic than where land and other interests in real property are concerned. It seemed interesting that this matter had been raised time and again at discussions about the implementation of land policy and more often than not dismissed with a vague reference to constitutional (or legal) "constraints" on the use of the power of taxation as an instrument of land planning policy.

During one of the early seminars of the Lincoln Institute of Land Policy in Cambridge, Massachusetts, the matter again came under discussion, and it seemed most appropriate at that time to do something concrete about the need to develop a better understanding of what those legal constraints really were. In other words, not just ad hoc determinations for given jurisdictions, but a reasonably complete summary of the kinds of limitations that were to be found in the various government jurisdictions throughout the country. This need has resulted in the initiation of a larger study of legal constraints of which this publication is the first part and the first published product.

To arrive at a fuller understanding of the legal framework under which the power of taxation operates as a regulatory device, it is necessary to understand the nature of both the federal and state taxing power and its sources. Thus the pertinent provisions of federal and state constitutions must be identified. This has in fact been the first step. Next, the related constitutional case law for each area needs to be identified, together with the all-important decisions dealing with the intergovernmental relationships and distributions of the taxing and police powers. The final and more extensive portion must deal with the statutory provisions at both the federal and state levels of government and the various delegations of the authority to tax (and regulate) as they apply to land and real property interests generally. Here, too, the related case law must be examined.

1 Background and Scope

Historical Background

The effort to guide land development in this country along the lines of preconceived government planning policy has met historically with some very unimpressive results. During the last several decades, when the idea of institutionalizing land planning began to take hold with certain seriousness, the question of the power to implement such policy within our legal and governmental framework came under more serious discussion.[1] Those who sought to establish the foundations of land planning in the United States were ultimately led to focus upon local government as the basic instrumentality for both defining and carrying out public policy.[2] To "effectuate" or "implement" *city* plans, the legal sources of municipal governmental powers were explored and enumerated.[3] The basic list was compiled: the power of eminent domain or condemnation with just compensation; the power to spend and withhold spending (including capital budgeting or phasing); the police power (which would include zoning, building and housing codes, subdivision regulations, and official "mapping" of streets and certain other public facilities to prevent conflicting construction); and last, the power of taxation. Suffice it to say that all of the first three categories were pursued vigorously at one time or another with rather spotty success. The last power, however—taxation—appears for the most part to have eluded the efforts of planning practitioners even to test its true efficacy as an instrument for the furtherance of land policy objectives. This state of affairs displays a great paradox, for while all other powers have been readily exercised and generally found wanting for the intended purpose, a great many planning professionals seem quite convinced that the one effective, even sufficient, power needed is that of taxation.

If this power has been so little used, why is this so? The most common way of answering this question has been to reply generally that there exist a number of constitutional and other legal constraints on the exercise of the taxing power for carrying out such purposes. Although this has been easy enough to say, it is hardly clear to most people working in areas concerned with land policy just what these various constraints ultimately amount to. It is therefore the purpose of this study to attempt to draw a legal profile of these constraints and to suggest what may reasonably be done to employ this basic instrument of government in the interests of better land usage.

1

Scope of the Study

Some preliminary thoughts are in order regarding the nature of the subject matter to be discussed. We have chosen to look at land as a matter of public policy concern and have chosen to examine taxation as a possible instrument for achieving desirable land-planning policies. The effort will be to focus more specifically on the legal constraints that exist on the use of the power of taxation for these purposes. Having said no more than this, some of the conceptual difficulties that face us become immediately apparent, and we certainly would not find them to be new in this discussion. The first difficulty, and ultimately the most troublesome, is the accretion of numerous social meanings and problems around the term *land*, which we continue to pretend is just a common physical substance marked out with simple geometric boundaries. In the practical effort to regulate land use, however, we are ultimately hard put to separate "land problems" from "social problems," and the unavoidable fact is that we cannot fully escape the merging of these many related matters in the one term. The second difficulty relates to the distinction between *land* and *improvements*, a differentiation for tax-assessment purposes that seems to have acquired a somewhat new significance in the realm of real property law beyond what it may have had historically.[4] A third problem, more directly related to the means, is just what is meant by the term *taxation*. A further investigation of the meaning of this term will necessarily bring us into the broader realm of government power and purpose.

Two more important implications thus become clear: we will have to study taxes other than land taxes to explore adequately the effects of taxation in relation to land policy, and we will have to go beyond tax collection to comprehend more fully the inherent regulatory effects of the general power of taxation.

There is yet another significant problem, not necessarily a conceptual one but one more commonly referred to as a question of causality: one of the greatest difficulties in the employment of any system of regulation is the basic need to establish adequately a causal relationship between the measure employed and the desired result. Uncertainty regarding the effect or impact of any tax measure has long pervaded the field of economics and finance, to say nothing of land policy and the broader concerns of public policy in general. I suspect that we will have to live for a long time with this uncertainty, and under no circumstances will this study pretend to deal with this "ultimate" question.

The basic approach of the study will be to examine constitutional (or "organic") law on the one hand, and legislative measures on the other, at the three levels of our government, together with the more important ex-

isting case law on the subject. In seeking to understand sources and limitations, rather than setting forth program narratives or an accounting, it is intended that the fullest scope for innovation may thereby be suggested.

Relationship to Law and Public Policy

The subject of public policy brings us to the current interest in policy
analysis and its relationship to the various historic efforts at legal reform.
Certainly this interest rightfully ought to extend to the area of taxation and
tax law. In any case, efforts to develop policy often have been concerned
with the "rationalization" of government actions and related legal
measures. However, in a thesis more fully developed elsewhere,[5] it has been
maintained that the impetus to "rationalize" laws in practical experience
has come about not so much as a "plan," which is then "carried out"
through various legal means, but as the need to understand the overall
"concert effect" of a proliferation of measures that have been adopted
more or less at random to deal with pressing needs or crisis situations. It
should not be surprising, therefore, if it were maintained that it is the existence of the contemporary government taxation establishment (at from
three to five levels of government), with its inherent policymaking
capabilities, that argues most for its rationalization, rather than any
abstract virtue that may lie in the "planning process." In this regard, most
authorities on the subject[6] seem to agree (1) that just about all taxes have
some regulatory effect (although it is not always clear just what that effect
is); (2) that regulatory functions are frequently carried out by various
governmental agencies and offices without public knowledge or appropriate
democratic involvement; and (3) that there are a host of tax measures that
simultaneously operate to encourage a given result (policy) on the one hand
and discourage it on the other. It seems hardly worth mentioning that
everyone finds undesirable consequences in the application of taxes; but this
might more hopefully be described as consensual doubt as to overall
benefits!
   It may thus be argued convincingly that a better understanding and use
of taxation as a regulatory device is more a matter of public self-defense
than the promotion of some evangelic purpose.[7] There is no area where this
conclusion is more justified than where the subject of land is concerned.

Notes

   1. See, Shurtleff and Olmsted, *Carrying Out the City Plan: The Practical Application of American Law in the Execution of City Plans* (1914).

2. See, for example, U.S. Department of Commerce, Advisory Committee on Building and Zoning, *Standard City Planning Enabling Act* (1928).

3. For a general review of early legal reference material relating to land planning, see Bernard, *The Development of a Body of City Planning Law*, 51 A.B.A.J. 632 (July 1965).

4. See 5 Powell *Real Property*, para. 660.

5. Bernard, *The Comprehensive Plan Concept as a Basis for Legal Reform*, 44 U. Det. J. Urban L. 611 (1967). Referring to Dean Pound's quotation in the conclusion of the article, one cannot help considering how Jefferson would have thought of "social architecture" rather than "social engineering."

6. Paul, *Taxation in the United States* (1954). See particularly pp. 650-654 therein. Griswold, *Federal Taxation* (6th ed. 1966), p. 52 and references cited therein. See generally Seligman, *Essays in Taxation* (10th ed. 1931) and *The Income Tax* (2nd ed. 1914).

7. Randolph Paul has commented: "It is fortunate that the Constitution does not deny to Congress the right to use the instrumentality of taxes for purposes beyond the revenue. With rates at present levels, it would be nothing short of madness to impose taxes for revenue only and with blind disregard for their social and economic consequences. Every tax is, in some measure, regulatory, since it interposes an economic impediment to the activity taxed as compared with other activities that are not taxed." *Supra* note 6, at 650.

2

Sources of the Taxing Power in General

Sources of the Federal Taxing Power

Before delving further into the relationships between public policy, land, and the taxing power, we should perhaps review briefly just what the organic sources of the taxing power in this country are. Beginning our investigations at the federal level, we recall that the U.S. Constitution grants enumerated powers to the federal government.[1] These enumerations more specifically refer to a distinct branch of government, intending separation from others.[2] The power to tax is thus granted to the legislative branch, and no other, under art. I., §8, cl. 1, of the Constitution,[3] and "... is a very extensive power. It is given in the Constitution with only one exception and only two qualifications. Congress cannot tax exports, and it must impose direct taxes by rule of apportionment, and indirect taxes by rule of uniformity. Thus limited, and thus only, it reaches every subject, and may be exercised at discretion."[4]

Constitutional Exceptions and Qualifications

The single exception mentioned by the U.S. Supreme Court refers to art. I, §9, cl. 5, dealing with exports, and is of little or no concern to us for the purposes of this investigation. The two qualifications mentioned are as follows. The first arises under art. I, §2, cl. 3, requiring that "Representatives and direct Taxes shall be apportioned among the several States which may be included within this Union, according to their respective Numbers . . . ,"[5] taken together with art. I, §9, cl. 4, requiring that "No Capitation, or other direct, Tax shall be laid, unless in Proportion to the Census or Enumeration herein before directed to be taken." This requirement of apportionment by numbers (census) is frequently said[6] to have been founded on the fear that the sparsely settled agricultural regions would have the tax burden shifted to them by the manufacturing states.[7] But Professor Seligman has shown it to be a virtual certainty that it was introduced simply and solely as a concession to slavery.[8]

The second qualification arises under the last portion of art. I, §8, cl. 1, "... but all Duties, Imposts and Excises shall be uniform throughout the United States." These are so-called indirect taxes, and it has been held that the requirement regarding them can be reliably fulfilled by simple unifor-

5

mity in the geographic sense,[9] or, stated another way, the tax must take no account of geography.[10]

Those who drafted the Constitution did not fully define the meaning of "direct" as opposed to "indirect" taxes.[11] What can be established is that at the time of ratification, land and capitation (poll) taxes were considered direct, and taxes such as those on income, gift, or inheritance did not exist in this country.[12] So we can never be quite sure how the founding fathers would have defined these latter taxes.[13] However, in practice, "direct" taxes were considered a last resort, when indirect taxes such as customs duties (then considered the fiscal mainstay) failed to produce sufficient revenue.[14]

The Income Tax and the Pollock Case

In later years, the increasing need for revenue, particularly for the Civil War, caused other taxes, such as the income tax, to come under consideration.[15] Under the Act of June 30, 1864,[16] a tax upon general income distributed uniformly throughout the United States was imposed and later unanimously upheld as an excise or indirect tax by the U.S. Supreme Court.[17] But a subsequent attempt to impose a tax on incomes uniformly throughout the United States under sections of the Wilson-Gorman Tariff Act, effective August 28, 1894,[18] was vigorously attacked and held to be unconstitutional by a severely divided Court in *Pollock v. Farmers' Loan & Trust Co.*[19] The details of this case are worth careful examination not only because the decision ultimately resulted in the enactment of the Sixteenth (Income Tax) Amendment to the Constitution, but also because the key issues responsible for this startling about-face by the Supreme Court are very closely related to the subject of land regulation to be discussed here. By judicially redefining the income tax from an indirect tax to a direct tax, the Court was able to impose the requirement of apportionment upon income taxes. It is important to note that, initially, the case centered on what was essentially a question of the *extent* of federal authority to tax *land*: if a tax on the *income of land* was permitted to be considered an excise or indirect tax, then land (that is, landed wealth) would effectively lose the "sheltering" advantage—as we term it today—that it had acquired as a result of the constitutional compromise recounted on the preceding page. This constraint, of course, is what would substantially limit any extensive attempt to adjust or shift the tax burden where the landlords would be concerned.[20]

To escape this evidently dreaded consequence, the Court was impelled to drag down the tax on income from personal property and income from labor, as well as the tax on rents and income from land, even though it expressly admitted that the tax on labor could have stood on its own without apportionment.[21] The opponents of income taxation (who were mainly in the wealthy manufacturing states) were thus able to use the apportionment clause to prevent the farming areas from requiring them to assume a fair share of the tax burden—a novel policy in any interpretation of its history.[22] The effect of the final decision in the *Pollock* case was to put most of the taxable wealth of the country beyond the reach of the federal government,[23] and as already indicated, ultimately resulted in the adoption of the Sixteenth (Income Tax) Amendment to the Constitution in 1913.

The Income Tax Amendment

This corrective amendment provided that "The Congress shall have the power to lay and collect taxes on incomes, from whatever source derived, without apportionment among the several States, and without regard to any census or enumeration." The wording, it was subsequently held, did not actually extend the taxing power of Congress to new subjects, but simply removed the necessity to apportion the income tax among the states. Furthermore, the phrase "from whatever source derived" was now definitely described as including income or rents from real estate but, interestingly, not state and municipal bonds.[24] Any direct federal land tax would still be subject to apportionment, and other taxes subsequently considered as direct by the Court[25] would presumably also be subject to that constraint.[26]

In holding the income tax to be a direct tax, the *Pollock* case created a serious interpretational difficulty for the Sixteenth Amendment. Because it was not an excise tax, the rule of uniformity did not apply, and with the removal by the amendment of the requirement of apportionment, an income tax would not be required to be either uniform *or* apportioned. Chief Justice White, in the *Brushaber* case, provided a solution to the matter, expressed in what must be one of the Court's more embarrassing sentences.[27]

By holding that the purpose of the amendment was only to relieve all income taxes from a consideration of the source whence the income was derived, the Court was able to convince itself that the rule of uniformity applied, to maintain some consistency with the *Pollock* case, and to lay to rest the troublesome possibility that a tax might be something else than either direct or indirect in nature.

If nothing else, the apportionment clause is a dramatic (if not bizarre) example of a legal measure in search of a policy. In any event, it has certainly known exceptional shifts from one objective to another, as has been previously indicated. And this is not to say that there is anything essentially "wrong" as such with direct taxation.[28]

Perhaps the most important assertions to be made by the Court during the testing of the newly enacted Sixteenth Amendment were that Congress is not precluded from leaving some incomes untaxed[29] and that, conversely, it may ". . . condition, limit or deny deductions from gross income to arrive at the net that it chooses to tax."[30]

It will be recalled that in the 1895 Income Tax, the exemption features of the Act, "the opening wedge," had been most bitterly attacked in the *Pollock* case.

Relationship of Fifth Amendment Due Process

While the Sixteenth Amendment relieves Congress of the requirement to apportion income taxes, the Fifth Amendment might still operate to forbid an obviously arbitrary classification from being imposed, by virtue of its "due process" clause.[31]

The application of due process and equal protection under the Fifth and Fourteenth Amendments with regard to taxation by the States and their instrumentalities will be discussed in chapter 5.

Effect of Judicial Redefinitions

During the period between the *Pollock* decision in 1895 and 1913, when the Sixteenth Amendment took effect, the Supreme Court evidently reacted to the growing threat to national solvency by "taking refuge in redefinitions."[32] This resulted in a federal tax on the privilege of doing business based on net corporate income being held to be indirect[33] and, also, in taxes such as those on inheritance being held to be excises. Thus, our current gift and estate taxes would be so defined and consequently would be treated as indirect in nature.[34] These newer federal taxes will also be of significance to our subsequent discussions regarding land policy.

Effect of "Reserved Powers" Provision

Further observations regarding the federal taxing power ought also to mention that the Tenth Amendment, reserving to the states or the people the powers not delegated to the United States by the Constitution or prohibited to the states, does not affect the taxing power, because that was specifically granted to Congress in the Constitution and was not reserved exclusively to the states.[35] Attempts to use the Tenth Amendment as a limitation to the federal taxing power in *Collector v. Day*[36] were subsequently expressly overruled in *Graves v. New York ex rel. O'Keefe*.[37]

Effect of "Necessary and Proper" Clause

Our concluding reference is to the fact that the power of taxation is the first of the enumerated powers contained in art. I, §8, of the Constitution, and, as such, must be read together with cl. 18, the last and so-called "necessary and proper" (or "coefficient") clause. The effect of this clause, "To make all Laws which shall be necessary and proper for carrying into Execution the foregoing Powers and all others Powers vested by this Constitution in the Government of the United States, or any Department or Officer thereof," is to add a "second dimension" to each of the "enumerated" powers of Congress.[38] The effect of this other dimension will become clear in our subsequent discussion of the decisions of the U.S. Supreme Court relating to the regulatory powers of taxation.

As a general rule, it may be said that most tax litigation does not involve constitutional questions, but when these issues are raised, the Court will defer ". . . where possible, to congressional procedures."[39]

Sources of the State Taxing Power

Let us now shift our investigation of the sources of the power of taxation to the states. It has already been indicated that the Tenth Amendment to the U.S. Constitution is not really a source of power as such. The thirteen original colonies were in fact independent sovereignties immediately prior to the ratification of the basic document in 1789, and where the power of taxation is concerned, it is abundantly clear that concurrent state and federal power was intended by the framers of the Constitution.[40] The later adoption of the Tenth Amendment as part of the Bill of Rights in 1791 was held in *U.S. v. Sprague*[41] ". . . to confirm the understanding of the people at the time the Constitution was adopted, that the powers not granted to the United States were reserved to the States or to the people. It added nothing to the instrument as originally ratified. . . ."

Taxation and Newly Admitted States

That there is a technical duality, however, regarding the source of the states' sovereign powers becomes evident with respect to cases decided under art. IV, §3, cl. 1, of the Constitution, dealing with the admission of new states to the Union. In general, a doctrine of equality or "equal footing"[42] has been adhered to, but there are notable exceptions. For example, in *Stearns v. Minnesota*,[43] the Supreme Court upheld a promise exacted from Minnesota upon its admission to the Union which was interpreted to limit its right to tax lands held by the United States at the time of admission and subsequently granted to a railroad. This case is also interesting for other reasons in that it introduces the perhaps surprising concept that sovereignty, in certain circumstances, may be contracted away, more particularly where taxation is concerned, a subject that will be treated more fully later.

Other important distinctions have arisen where new states are concerned, with regard to rights to or jurisdiction over lands under water.[44]

Derivation, Delegation, and Separation of Powers

Questions relating to the derivation of state sovereignty will perhaps always be with us. Be that as it may, the states' sovereign power to tax is individually defined by, but not derived from, the constitutions of each of the fifty states that are currently members of the Union.[45] At this writing, there are, in fact, at least fifty-one constitutions defining and circumscribing such powers, since the Commonwealth of Puerto Rico has associated itself with the United States under a compact relationship,[46] adopting its own constitution on July 25, 1952.

The state power of taxation has been exercised in this country either by the state (or commonwealth) directly enacting legislation through its legislative body under its particular constitution, or under a constitutional or statutory delegation that has typically taken three forms: (1) to a municipality as such; (2) to a county; or (3) to a special-purpose entity with a related taxing district. All of these may be designated municipal corporations by a state for general legal purposes. However, express language of delegation from the state has been required by the courts to sustain the exercise of the power of taxation by a municipal corporation.[47]

The "separation of powers" doctrine has been held to be inapplicable to the states as a requirement of federal constitutional law.[48] Thus, the individual state constitutional provisions must be looked to for specific provisions on this subject and related judicial interpretations. See chapter 6 and table 9.

Notes

1. The doctrine is expounded by Justice Marshall in *McCulloch v. Maryland*, 4 Wheat. 316, 405 (1819), where, curiously, the groundwork is also laid for the many exceptions that are to follow.

2. U.S. Constitution arts. I, II, and III.

3. "The Congress shall have Power to lay and collect Taxes, Duties, Imposts and Excises, to pay the Debts and provide for the common Defence

and general Welfare of the United States; but all Duties, Imposts and Excises shall be uniform throughout the United States." (Constitutional quotations are taken from the Literal Print throughout.)

4. *License Tax Cases*, 5 Wall. 462, 471 (1867).

5. The remaining portion of the clause, effectively changed by the Fourteenth Amendment, reads as follows: ". . . which shall be determined by adding to the whole Number of free Persons, including those bound to Service for a Term of Years, and excluding Indians not taxed, three fifths of all other Persons."

6. Ratner, *American Taxation* (1942); see particularly p. 19 therein.

7. This historical conception (or misconception) has been repeated by many legal writers both without and within the judicial system, but is mostly traceable, as will be seen, to recent origins.

8. Seligman, *The Income Tax* (2d ed., 1914), see particularly pp. 531-559. See also Bullock, *The Origin, Purpose and Effect of the Direct Tax Clause of the Federal Constitution*, 15 Pol. Sci. Q. 217, 452 (1900).

In order to break the deadlock on the issue of whether or not to count slaves for purposes of representation in Congress, Gouverneur Morris at the 1787 Federal Convention in Philadelphia moved to tie taxation to representation, so that both sides (slave states and free states) would find an incentive to accept the fractional compromise that had been earlier proposed by Madison in the Continental Congress resolution of April 18, 1783 (that is, "three fifths of all other Persons"), ultimately to be found in the last portion of art. I, §2, cl. 3, of the adopted Constitution. In order to avoid the criticism that was then raised by Mr. Mason of Virginia that Congress might be forced by such wording to resort to the practice of "requisitions," Morris agreed to restrict the language to "direct taxes" only.

The similar phrasing of art. I, §9, cl. 4, had a somewhat different though related history. Here, the "capitation clause" was tied to an apportionment based on the census to prevent an arbitrary tax from being imposed on slaves by the northern majority. The subsequent addition of the words "or other direct tax" was then accepted on the motion of Mr. Read of Delaware, for the purpose of preventing the old "requisitions" due from the delinquent states under the Confederacy from later being collected.

Madison's personal notes on these matters are found in 5 Elliot, *Debates on the Adoption of the Federal Constitution in the Convention held at Philadelphia in 1787; with a Diary of the Debates of the Congress of the Confederation; as reported by James Madison, a Member and Deputy from Virginia* (1845); see particularly pp. 79-80, 302, 304, 309, 315, 363, 392, 393, and 545 therein.

Those who doubt the realities of the compromise described might do well to consider what happened directly after the passage of the Thirteenth Amendment in 1865, freeing the slaves. It was found that now each still-voteless black was to be counted as a whole person under art. I, §2, cl. 3, increasing the Southern white representation by two-fifths of the black population. The Fourteenth Amendment only partially corrected for this, over two and one-half years later; it took the Fifteenth Amendment, almost four and one-half years later, to deal with the problem.

9. In *Knowlton v. Moore*, 178 U.S. 41 (1900), upholding a federal inheritance tax on legacies, the Court stated: "The tax is hence uniform throughout the United States, despite the fact that different conditions among the states may obtain" (that is, producing varying amounts of revenue).

In *Bromley v. McCaugh*, 280 U.S. 124 (1929), upholding the federal gift tax, the Court also stated: "While taxes levied upon or collected from persons because of their general ownership of property may be taken to be direct, this court has consistently held, almost from the foundation of government, that a tax imposed upon a particular use of property incidental to ownership, is an excise which need not be apportioned." Thus: "The uniformity of taxation throughout the United States enjoined by article I, §8 is geographic, not intrinsic."

In *Fernandez v. Wiener*, 326 U.S. 340 (1945), reh. den. 327 U.S. 814, upholding the federal estate tax, the Court explained: ". . . a tax is uniform when it operates with the same force and effect in every place where the subject of it is found. The amendment taxing community property interests is applicable throughout the territory of the United States wherever such interests may be found. There is no lack of geographical uniformity because in some states they are not found. For a taxing statute does not fall short of the prescribed uniformity because its operation and incidence may be affected by differences in state laws."

10. In *Florida v. Mellon*, 273 U.S. 12 (1927), the Court upheld a federal inheritance tax that provided for a credit of up to 80 percent for a similar tax that was actually paid to any state or territory; even though Florida did not levy such a tax, this was not found to violate the requirement of geographical uniformity.

11. At the 1787 Federal Convention in Philadelphia, when the taxing clause came before the Convention for final action, Mr. King of Massachusetts asked "what was the precise meaning of *direct* taxation?" Madison here recorded, "no one answered." Elliot, *supra* note 8 at 451.

12. Ratner, *supra* note 6.

13. Professor Seligman, after a review of authorities of international scope, concludes that "there are almost as many classifications . . . as there are authors." He also shows quite clearly that, historically, there has been no relationship between economic and constitutional definitions of direct and indirect taxes. *Supra* note 8 at 433-440.

14. See *History of the Internal Revenue Service, 1791-1929*, (Bureau of

Internal Revenue, 1930). See also Surrey & Warren, *Federal Income Taxation* (1961 ed.), in particular p. 2.

15. For a historic review of the early attempts at taxation in the United States, see Paul, *Taxation in the United States, supra* chapter 1, note 6. particularly chapter I therein.

16. 13 Stat. 223, 281 (1864).

17. *Springer v. U.S.*, 102 U.S. 586 (1881). See also *Pacific Insurance Co. v. Soule*, 7 Wall. 433 (1869), upholding a 1864 tax on an insurance company's receipts for premiums and assessments as an "excise," or indirect tax; and *Hylton v. U.S.*, 3 Dall. 171 (1796), the so-called "Carriage Tax" case, expressing strong opinions that only land and poll taxes were intended to be considered "direct." Justice Iredell, for example (in the *seriatim* opinion), stated, "As all direct taxes must be apportioned, it is evident that the Constitution contemplated none as direct, but such as could be apportioned. If this cannot be apportioned, it is, therefore, not a direct tax in the sense of the Constitution." This was the first case to consider the constitutionality of an act of Congress.

18. 28 Stat. 509, 553 (1894).

19. 157 U.S. 429 (1895); reh. 158 U.S. 601 (1895).

20. It would be an error to conclude from this that progressivity is totally precluded by the use of direct taxation at the federal level. In the first attempt at direct taxation in 1798, land was taxed at a fixed rate on assessed value, slaves were taxed at 50 cents per slave, but dwellings were taxed on a progressive rate schedule in nine classes ranging from assessed values of $100 to $30,000. When the Bill that ultimately resulted in this Act was before the U.S. House of Representatives, Mr. Holmes of Virginia ". . . rose to observe, that an idea had struck him that a part of this law does not altogether accord with the Constitution which says: 'No capitation or direct tax shall be laid, unless in proportion to the census or enumeration of the inhabitants of the United States,' as it supposes that the proposed tax on houses and slaves may exceed the whole of the tax apportioned to a State, in which case the surplus is to be paid into the Treasury of the United States, and placed to the credit of such State; and though a provision is made for crediting the said State with the surplus money, he did not believe that would be strictly conformable to the Constitution; since it would have the operation of a forced loan upon a State which should be so circumstanced, which would not be warranted by the Constitution." Representative Harper, in order to remove the constitutional objection pointed out, moved to insert the following: "If, in making the assessment of any State, it shall appear that the amount to be collected from houses and slaves, will exceed the sum apportioned to such State, then the Supervisor shall be authorized to deduct from the tax on houses such rate as to confine it within the limits of the said apportionment." This motion was then carried. 8 *Annals of*

Congress 2060-1 (1798). In the final version of the Act, this provision was to read as follows: "And the whole amount of the sums so to be assessed upon dwelling-houses and slaves within each state respectively, shall be deducted from the sum hereby apportioned to such state, and the remainder of the said sum shall be assessed upon the lands within such state according to the valuations to be made pursuant to the act aforesaid, and at such rate per centum as will be sufficient to produce the said remainder." Act of July 14, 1798, 1 Stat. 597, ch. 75, §2. For a current discussion of this subject, see Soltow, *America's First Progressive Tax*, 30 Natl. Tax J. 53 (March, 1977). Upon analysis, Soltow finds the 1798 Act to be one of the best examples of tax-structure design from the point of view of equitableness and mathematical precision!

There were five attempts by Congress to lay and apportion direct taxes on property, the first being the Act of July 14, 1798, 1 Stat. 597, ch. 75, also the Act of July 9, 1798, *id*. 580, ch. 70, assessing same; the Act of August 2, 1813, 3 Stat. 53, ch. 37, also the Act of January 22, 1813, *id*. 22, ch. 16; the Act of January 9, 1815, 3 Stat. 164, ch. 21; the Act of March 5, 1816, 3 Stat. 255, ch. 24; and the final one, the Act of August 5, 1861, 12 Stat. 292, 294, ch. 45, during the Civil War. This last tax was levied on real property and household furnishings and apportioned to include the states that had seceded from the Union. Its collection proved to be so frustrating that in 1891 Congress was to reimburse all the states that had already paid and abandon the effort. Act of March 2, 1891, ch. 496.

21. In the first hearing of the case, the Court held that if a tax on real estate was direct, then a tax on the income of real estate must also be direct. It did not choose to decide the other questions propounded in the appeal, which were as follows: (1) whether the provisions of the Act declared unconstitutional invalidated all the income tax provisions; (2) whether the tax on income from personal property was a direct tax and hence unconstitutional; (3) whether any part of the tax, if not considered a direct tax, would be invalid as offending against the rule of uniformity. See 157 U.S. at 429.

The opinion in the first hearing resulted in so much confusion to all concerned that it was appealed by both parties, and a second hearing was granted. Again the Court held that a tax on rents or income from real estate was a direct tax and was unconstitutional unless apportioned. In an attempt to maintain some consistency, it also decided to include income from personal property within its reasoning. The whole Court agreed, however, that taxes on income from professions, trades, employments, or vocations were valid as being in the nature of excises. However, the five justices who had voted against validity held that the entire Act must fall, because, among other things, the resultant burdens would then be unfairly placed. See 158 U.S. at 601.

In their zeal to prevent the march of "communistic," "socialistic," and "populist" principles, counsel for the plaintiffs involved the high court in what were evidently a number of serious misinterpretations of history.

Joseph Choate, in particular, convinced a sufficient number of the Justices that the direct tax clauses had been the result of a historic compromise designed to protect the richer states against the poorer: "... there was a surrender by the States to Congress of the exclusive power to levy taxes on imports . . . Then, too, the States surrendered forever afterwards the right they had had of taxing and regulating commerce between the States . . .Then came the grant to Congress of power to lay indirect taxes, as we now call them." All these were an "essential part of the compromise" whereby the power of the federal government to levy taxes was restricted. The rule of apportionment also resulted "in a law of protection for the benefit of the holder of such property as was contemplated as the subject of direct taxes . . . There had occurred an accumulation of wealth *per capita* in certain states to a greater extent than in other states . . . It was just this disproportion that the provision as to apportionment was intended to protect . . . It was then understood perfectly well to be a rule of inequality, on the strength of which was bought the assent of the States then owning such property . . . The question . . . is whether that bargain shall be repudiated. Your Honors know what the seaboard States gave up for it. . . ." 157 U.S. 543.

Justice Field repeated the inaccuracies in his opinion: "The States bordering on the ocean were unwilling to give up their rights to lay duties on imports, which were their chief source of revenue. The other States, on the other hand, were unwilling to make any agreement for the levying of taxes directly upon real and personal property, the smaller States fearing that they would be overbourne by unequal burdens forced upon them by the action of the larger States . . . But happily a compromise was effected by an agreement that direct taxes should be laid by Congress by apportioning them. . . ." 157 U.S. 587.

This was restated in the second opinion on rehearing as follows: "The States, respectively . . . gave up the great sources of revenue derived from commerce; . . . they retained the power of direct taxation, and to that they look as their chief resource; but even in respect of that they granted the concurrent power . . . Therefore, they did not grant the power of direct taxation without regard to their own condition and resources as States . . . If, in the changes of wealth and population in particular States, apportionment produced inequality, it was an inequality stipulated for, just as the equal representation of the States, however small, in the Senate, was stipulated for." 158 U.S. 620. Professor Seligman comments: "In the light of history . . . all of these statements must be characterized as essentially erroneous." *Supra* note 8 at 557-559. See also Paul, *supra* chapter 1, note 6, at 40-64.

Among other things, counsel also misrepresented to the Court that the framers of the Constitution had had a clear understanding of the distinction between direct and indirect taxes.

22. *Supra* note 6.

23. Seligman, *supra* note 8.

24. *Brushaber v. Union Pacific Railroad Co.*, 240 U.S. 1 (1916). See also *Stanton v. Baltic Mining Co.*, 240 U.S. 103 (1916).

25. That the Court was tacitly willing to consider the definition as open-ended, see *Brushaber v. Union Pacific Railroad Co.*, *id.* at 18-19; *Stanton v. Baltic Mining Co.*, *id.* at 112. See also Corwin, *The Constitution* (13th ed., 1973) at 437.

26. The Congressional procedures involved in complying with the Constitutional apportionment requirement for direct taxes in general would appear to be: (a) a decision as to the nature of the tax to be levied (that is, property or poll); (b) a determination of the amount to be raised; (c) an assignment to each state of a quota based upon the last census share of the population; and (d) provision for assessment and collection of the tax within each state in keeping with the assigned quotas. It can be seen that widely different tax rates for different states are quite possible. Examples of possible disparities are cited in Seligman, *supra* note 8 at 587 and 599.

27. Justice White explained: "Moreover, in addition, the conclusion reached in the *Pollock Case* did not in any degree involve holding that income taxes generically and necessarily come within the class of direct taxes on property, but, on the contrary, recognized the fact that taxation on income was in its nature an excise entitled to be enforced as such unless and until it was concluded that to enforce it would amount to accomplishing the result which the requirement as to apportionment of direct taxation was adopted to prevent, in which case the duty would arise to disregard form and consider substance alone, and hence subject the tax to the regulation as to apportionment which otherwise as an excise would not apply to it." The all-important "result" referred to that had to be prevented was earlier stated in the opinion as follows: ". . . that the classification of direct was adopted for the purpose of rendering it impossible to *burden by taxation accumulations of property*, real or personal, except subject to the regulation of apportionment" (emphasis added), 240 U.S. at 16-17.

28. Professor Seligman comments:"Direct taxation, as we have seen, generally forms the last step in the historical development of public revenues." *Essays in Taxation* (10th ed., 1931) at 6.

Efforts to remove the words *direct taxes* from the Constitution or to word the Sixteenth Amendment so that Congress would have the power to lay and collect direct taxes without apportionment were disposed of with inadequate discussion. See 44 Cong. Rec. 4109, 4120 (1909). See also Seligman, *supra* note 8 at 595-596. "We have learned that the only reason of its original insertion was to effect a compromise on the slavery question. Now that slavery had long been abolished, there was no further reason for retaining the clause in the Constitution." *id.* at 594.

29. *Brushaber v. Union Pacific Railroad Co.*, *supra* note 24. Other

extremely important principles for income taxation upheld by the decision were as follows: (a) retroactivity; (b) progressive taxation; (c) tax exemption of specified organizations; (d) distinctions between corporate and individual taxation; (e) deductions and exemptions based on income; (f) exemptions based on cohabitation and marital status; (g) discrimination between different classes of corporations and individuals with regard to deductions and limitation of deductions; (h) withholding at source; (i) no income imputed from the rental value of homes; (j) no income imputed from farm produce consumed by farmer; (k) no deductions for rents paid on leased homes. These matters were in the main attacked on the basis of Fifth Amendment due-process grounds, which will be discussed further.

30. *Helvering v. Independent L. Ins. Co.*, 292 U.S. 371, 381 (1934); *Helvering v. Winmill*, 305 U.S. 79, 84 (1938).

31. Corwin, *The Constitution* (14th ed., 1978) at 542; 2 Antieau, *Modern Constitutional Law*, §12:45. See also *Heiner v. Donnan*, 285 U.S. 312 (1932), where a conclusive presumption of transfer in contemplation of death (two years) was held to violate due process (death transfer tax under Act of February 26, 1926, 44 Stat. 70, §302); Cf. *Fernandez v. Weiner, supra* note 9, upholding estate tax on community property.

In *Stewart Machine Co. v. Davis*, 301 U.S. 548 (1937), upholding the Social Security Act tax, Justice Cardozo commented: ". . . discrimination, if gross enough, is equivalent to confiscation and subject under the Fifth Amendment to challenge and annulment." This is to be compared with Justice White's statement in the *Brushaber* case: "So far as the due process clause of the 5th Amendment is relied upon, it suffices to say that there is no basis for such reliance, since it is equally well settled that such clause is not a limitation upon the taxing power conferred upon Congress by the Constitution; in other words, that the Constitution does not conflict with itself by conferring, upon the one hand, a taxing power, and taking the same power away, on the other, by the limitations of the due process clause . . . And no change in the situation here would arise even if it be conceded, as we think it must be, that this doctrine would have no application in a case where, although there was a seeming exercise of the taxing power, the act complained of was so arbitrary as to constrain to the conclusion that it was not the exertion of taxation, but a confiscation of property; that is, a taking of the same in violation of the 5th Amendment; or, what is equivalent thereto, was so wanting in basis for classification as to produce such a gross and patent inequality as to inevitably lead to the same conclusion." 240 U.S. at 24-25, and cases cited therein. In *U.S. v. Manufacturers National Bank*, 363 U.S. 194 (1960), the Court stated that ". . . it cannot be held that the tax offends due process . . . [unless it is shown] . . . that the lawmakers did a wholly arbitrary thing, or that they found equivalence where there was none, or that they laid a burden unrelated to privilege or benefit."

As to whether taxation may be considered a "taking" under the Fifth and Fourteenth Amendments, see page 49 and accompanying notes.

In *Detroit Bank v. U.S.,* 317 U.S. 329 (1943), the Court noted: "Unlike the XIV amend., the V amend. contains no equal protection clause and it provides no guarantee against discrimination by Congress."

32. Corwin, *supra* note 31 at 540-541, and cases cited therein.

33. *Flint v. Stone Tracy,* 220 U.S. 107 (1911).

34. *Knowlton v. Moore; Bromley v. McCaugh, supra* note 9. There was, however, earlier precedent in the Civil War succession tax (Act of June 30, 1864, 13 Stat. 281) being upheld as indirect and not requiring apportionment in *Scholey v. Rew,* 23 Wall. 331 (1875).

35. In *The License Cases,* 5 How. 504, 588 (1847), the principle was stated as follows: "The power to tax is common to the federal and state governments, and it may be exercised by each in taxing the same property. . . ."

36. 11 Wall. 113 (1871), holding the salary of a state judge exempt from federal income taxation.

37. 306 U.S. 466 (1939), where the reverse situation occurred, and the income of an employee of the Home Owners' Loan Corp., a federal agency, was held subject to New York State taxation. The relationship of the doctrine of federal supremacy in these cases will be discussed in chapter 5 herein. See also, *Fernandez v. Wiener, supra* note 9. The Court there stated: "The X amend. does not operate as a limitation upon the powers, expressed or implied, delegated to the national government." Cf. *National League of Cities v. Usery,* 426 U.S. 833 (1976), holding federal wage and hour regulation of state and local government invalid, and *Massachusetts v. U.S.,* 435 U.S. 444 (1978), holding federal user fee valid as applied to state police helicopter.

38. Corwin, *supra* note 31 at 38.

39. *Schlude v. C.I.R.,* 372 U.S. 128 (1963), *American Auto. Assoc. v. U.S.,* 367 U.S. 687 (1961).

40. *The Federalist,* Nos. 32-34 (Hamilton). (With the single exception of the tax on imports, under art. I, §10, cl. 2, which was prohibited to the states without the consent of Congress, unless absolutely necessary for executing inspection laws. Both state and federal governments are prohibited from taxing exports under this clause taken together with art. I, §9, cl. 5.)

A discussion by Justice Marshall of the distinction between exclusive and concurrent powers (re commerce and taxation) is contained in *Gibbons v. Ogden,* 9 Wheat. 1 (1824).

41. 282 U.S. 716, 733 (1931). In *The License Cases, supra* note 35 at 587, the Court had declared: "Before the adoption of the Constitution, the States possessed, respectively, all the attributes of sovereignty. In their organic laws they had distributed their powers of government according to their own views, subject to such modifications as the people of each State might sanction."

42. In *U.S. v. Texas*, 143 U.S. 621, 634 (1892), it was held that the Joint Resolution of December 29, 1845, 9 Stat. 108, had provided that Texas ". . . was admitted into the Union on an equal footing with the original States in all respects whatever."

In *Coyle v. Smith*, 221 U.S. 559 (1911), the Congressional Enabling Act of 1906 providing for the admission of Oklahoma stipulated that the state capital should be temporarily located at Guthrie and not changed prior to 1913, with no money appropriated except as necessary for capitol buildings until that time. The U.S. Supreme Court sustained a 1910 Act of Oklahoma removing the capital to Oklahoma City and appropriating money for capitol buildings, stating that these were essentially state powers, and referring to the principles of equality with the original states.

43. 179 U.S. 223, 245 (1900).

44. In *Pollard v. Hagan*, 3 How. 212, 223 (1845), the U.S. Supreme Court held that the original states had reserved to themselves the ownership of the shores of navigable waters and the soils beneath, and that title passes to the new state upon admission under the doctrine of equality. However, in *U.S. v. California*, 332 U.S. 19 (1947), the Court refused to extend the rule to the three-mile belt. See also *U.S. v. Louisiana*, 339 U.S. 669 (1950). In *U.S. v. Texas*, 339 U.S. 699, 707, 716 (1950), where Texas, in distinction to the original states, did in fact own the soil under the three-mile belt prior to annexation to the United States, it was held that dominion and sovereignty were surrendered over it upon entry into the Union on terms of equality with existing states! This modified the rule set down in *Brown v. Grant*, 116 U.S. 207 (1886), that unless otherwise declared by Congress, the title to every species of property owned by a territory passes to the state upon admission to the Union. Yet when the Submerged Land Act of 1953, 43 U.S.C. 1311, was passed, turning over to the states title to and ownership of the lands beneath navigable waters within the boundaries of the respective states, including lands covered by tidal waters up to three miles seaward and to the boundary line of each such state, ". . . where in any case as it existed at the time such State became a member of the Union . . . extends seaward (or into the Gulf of Mexico) beyond three geographical miles," the Supreme Court refused to upset the Act as violating the "equal-footing" doctrine, simply reaffirming the power of Congress to dispose of any kind of property belonging to the United States without limitation. *Alabama v. Texas*, 347 U.S. 272 (1954).

45. See McQuillin, *Municipal Corporations*, §44.05 (3d ed., 1972): "The power to tax inheres in the state as an attribute of its sovereignty, and is not dependent upon a grant of power in the constitution. Constitutional provisions relating to taxation are not grants of power, but limitations upon the exercise of a power necessarily possessed by every sovereign state. Except as restricted by such provisions, the power of the state to tax is unlimited."

46. P.L. 600, 81st Cong., Act of July 3, 1950, ch. 446, 64 Stat. 320; Congressional approval, July 3, 1952, P.L. 447, 82nd Cong.; 48 U.S.C.

731. The federal power of taxation is limited with respect to Puerto Rico as a matter of Congressional policy. *R.C.A. v. Gov't. of the Capital*, 91 P.R.R. 404 (1964); P.L. 600, *supra*. In not choosing to be admitted as a state under art. IV, §3, cl. 1, Puerto Rico has no voting representative in Congress. Its citizens are citizens of the United States by virtue of prior acts of Congress, and are entitled to full protection of the Constitution including the Fourteenth Amendment. However, as pointed out in the *R.C.A.* case, *supra*, there are differences regarding restrictions on taxation of interstate commerce. See Corwin, *supra* note 31 at 214-216, regarding Congressional powers under art. IV, §3, cl. 2, where former territories are concerned. Other territories, such as the Northern (Pacific) Marianas, have recently taken similar steps toward Commonwealth status. See Covenant to Establish Constitution, P.L. 94-241, March 24, 1976, 90 Stat. 263 (art. VI deals with powers of taxation); 48 U.S.C.A., §1681 *et seq.*

47. "Municipal corporations have no inherent power of taxation. On the contrary, municipal corporations possess with respect to taxation only such power as has been granted to them by the constitution or the statutes."

". . . [S]ince the authority to levy taxes is an extraordinary one, it should never be left to implication unless it be a necessary implication . . . if there is a doubt as to the existence of the power, such doubt will be resolved against the municipality and in favor of the taxpayer." McQuillin, *Municipal Corporations, supra* note 45.

48. *Dreyer v. Illinois*, 187 U.S. 71, 83-84 (1902). It is through the due process clause of the Fourteenth Amendment that the federal courts must find authority to review the delegation by state legislatures of power to others which the legislature might have exercised directly. See *Eubank v. City of Richmond*, 226 U.S. 137 (1912); *Embree v. Kansas City Road District*, 240 U.S. 242 (1916).

3 The Nature of the Taxing Power

Classification of Taxation

No discussion of the theoretical bases of the taxing power would be complete without reference to Professor Seligman's essay *The Classification of Public Revenues*.[1] After distinguishing the sources of public revenue as gratuitous, contractual, and compulsory, he sets about examining in particular the nature of the last category in terms of the essential aspects of government sovereignty. Property may be taken from individuals by the state in several enumerated ways: (1) by eminent domain;[2] (2) by the police power; (3) by the penal power; or (4) by the power of taxation. It is interesting to note that a specific division has been made here between "police power" and "penal power"; we more often tend to find all "regulatory" powers lumped together under the general title of "police powers." But an important difference in their nature is emphasized by the separate terminology. The more extreme acts of sovereignty, otherwise technically known as the "power of sanction," while often producing substantial revenue from fines and penalties for certain acts or omissions, nevertheless cross the legal boundary line into the area of criminal law or penology.[3] Where this is the case, they are made subject to a somewhat different set of legal standards. More specifically, under the U.S. Constitution we find the provisions of the Eighth Amendment governing federal actions with the requirement that "Excessive bail shall not be required, or excessive fines imposed, nor cruel and unusual punishments inflicted." This provision has since been held to be incorporated into the scope of the Fourteenth Amendment, applying to actions by the States[4] (and, by extension, to their instrumentalities, the municipal governments).

A more important discussion of distinctions follows regarding the police power and the taxing power. Professor Seligman's considerable stature as a scholar makes his initial statement on the subject all the more provocative: ". . . it may be confidently stated that from the standpoint of the science of finance the distinction drawn between the police power and the taxing power is to a great extent a fiction, referable to certain difficulties in American constitutional law and to a lack of economic analysis on the part of the judges . . ."[5]

While some theorists have refused to grant the name *tax* to any measure that looks to a purpose other than taxation for revenue, and Judge Cooley, in his treatise[6] would have looked, in the alternative, to the "primary purpose" (that is, regulation or revenue) of a given fiscal measure to determine whether it was an exercise of the police power or the power to tax, Professor Seligman forcefully shows that common measures that are primarily regulatory in intent have nonetheless long been accepted as taxes. For example, protective import duties, a 10 percent tax on state bank notes, imposed with the obvious purpose of destroying such issues, and extraordinary taxes on colored as opposed to uncolored oleomargarine, on liquor, and on certain addictive drugs, have all been so accepted.[7]

He is also able to demonstrate (with particular reference to the state level of government) how the courts have tended to make the police/taxing power distinction mainly on a public policy basis, bending their definitions to satisfy the particular statutory or constitutional limitation concerned. He thus observed: "Anyone who has studied the American law of taxation as a whole must have become painfully conscious of the hopeless contradictions among the laws of the several states on many important points. This condition is due in a great measure to the fact that the constitution or laws of one state by implication forbid what the constitution or laws of another state expressly permit. In order to take an actual case, which is perhaps in line with public policy, out of the range of the legal inhibition, the courts of the first state are forced to adopt an interpretation wholly unnecessary in the second. Thus the continuity of social development is preserved, even at the sacrifice of legal consistency or uniformity. For instance, in New York street-car licenses are held to fall under the taxing power, while in Pennsylvania they are put under the police power, simply because, under the particular conditions, it seemed to be a matter of equity, in the one case to uphold, and in the other to object to, such charge.[8] The payment in the two instances was the same, both in amount and in principle; but the attempt to make the same laws conform to a public policy which differs in the different states has brought about a contradiction. So, too, the whole system of high license or liquor taxes is in some states brought under the taxing power; but in others, because of certain constitutional difficulties, is put under the police power.[9] To this extent the police power has been a legal fiction to enable the courts to uphold what could not well be brought under the taxing power; although in another leading case[10] the liquor tax was upheld under the taxing power because there was a constitutional obstacle to its being put under the licensing or police power. The police power is of great and growing legal importance in the United States, largely because of the peculiar principles of American governmental relations, whereby local bodies are deemed to have only those powers expressly delegated to them, in contradistinction to the European method according to which local bodies possess, in certain respects, all powers not expressly withheld from them."[11]

His most significant analysis comes with his exposition of what he terms the "taxing power in the wider sense," as distiguished from a "tax in the narrow sense." The taxing power in the wider sense would include: (1) taxes in the narrow sense, such as those imposed on the means or faculty of the taxpayer; (2) fees, such as those imposed for licenses and legal documents, and for the use of the courts; and (3) special assessments, as for utility installations on land. In common, they are all compulsory contributions levied for the support of government, or to defray the expenses incurred for public purposes. The distinctions are made as follows: a tax in the narrow sense is levied as a part of a common burden; a fee is assessed as a payment for a special privilege. The basis of a fee is a special measurable benefit accruing to the individual. The basis of a tax in the narrow sense is the ability or faculty of the taxpayer; the benefit is not susceptible to direct measurement. In the case of the fee, the particular advantage is the very reason of the payment; in the case of the tax, the advantage, if it exists at all, is simply an incidental result of the state action. Fees do not normally exceed the cost of service to an individual. Where they are permitted to do so, this ultimately amounts to their conversion into a special tax. Where fees are reduced to below cost, the service is in turn ultimately converted into a general benefit. Because fees are not taxes in the narrow sense, they should not necessarily be considered police-power regulations. The true distinction between fees and taxes in the narrow sense can be clearly demonstrated to be nothing more than one of special or common benefit: "A tax is no less a tax because its purpose is regulation or destruction; and a fee or payment for regulation brings in just as much revenue as a precisely identical fee imposed primarily for revenue. From the standpoint of finance the test is not whether the payment is for regulation, but . . . whether it is primarily for special benefit or primarily for common benefit; that is, it is a distinction not between police power and taxing power, but between fees and taxes."[12] In other words, both fees and taxes may be employed for either regulatory or revenue-raising purposes.

Special assessments, on the other hand, are compulsory contributions levied in proportion to the special benefits derived, to defray the costs of a specific improvement to real property undertaken in the public interest. The element of public purpose must always be present; it must be capable of apportionment; there must be an assessment area over which the whole assessment is levied, to be then further distributed according to a definite rule of apportionment,[13] and the assessment must not be arbitrary. Special assessments, like fees, relate to services that redound to the particular benefit of the individual, in distinction to taxes in the narrow sense. Special taxes, in distinction, such as those relating to fire or police protection in some communities, are still levied on the basis of the "means" or "faculty" of the taxpayer. In special assessment, the benefit both is measurable and forms the basis of the levy. While taxes may be made either proportional or progressive, special assessments cannot be made to be progressive. They have also been held to be voidable where the charge exceeds the special benefit.[14] However, the use of acreage, frontage, and value have all been upheld as proper guides to apportionment and as constitutional tests of presumptive special benefit.[15] The sphere of special assessments is limited to local improvements; the sphere of fees and taxes is generally unlimited. Special assessments, like fees, require a specific service to be performed. Special assessments, unlike taxes, are specially confined to increasing the capital account of the community.

The "Institutional Economics" Movement

A most interesting movement in the field of economics occurred in this country during the 1920s and 1930s, drawing its inspiration perhaps most heavily from the work of the economist Thorstein Veblen. It included among its followers Rexford Tugwell, the Roosevelt New Deal "Brain-truster," Professor John R. Commons of the University of Wisconsin, and, in England, Sidney and Beatrice Webb. Referred to generally as *Institutional Economics*, the movement viewed the evolution of economic institutions as part of a broader process of cultural development. Professor Commons, in particular, produced some significant legal analyses of government economic powers under our constitutional form of government.[16] Unquestionably influenced by Professor Seligman's work, he asks:

> Shall we look at a tax, or taxation in general, from the standpont of what has happened in the past, or from the standpoint of what will happen in the future as an effect of the tax? If we look at it from the standpoint of what has previously happened, then we shall emphasize equality, ability to pay, the original or free gifts of nature, the accidents of good luck—in short, the dollars obtained in the past—as the proper measure of taxes; and we shall quite properly look upon income taxes, inheritance taxes, or the uniform property tax on accumulations of the past, as the appropriate method of taxation. But if we look at a tax from the police-power standpoint of what may be expected as the economic results of the tax, then we shall inquire: What will be the best inducements to individuals to increase the commonwealth by increasing their own wealth? This is what we name the police power of taxation. The police power looks to the future; the taxing power looks to the past and to the accumulations from the past.

> Indeed, it is well recognized that taxes and tax exemptions operate like the police power, and are often consciously employed for the regulation of industry, morals, or welfare, rather than the acquisition of public revenue. Professor Seligman has shown that the American distinction between the taxing power and the police power is, to a great extent, a legal fiction growing out of our system of government, and is unnecessary from the economic and fiscal standpoint. Furthermore, we may add, under the deci-

sions of our courts, taxation is a somewhat privileged exercise of the police power, since, considering that it is the principal means of collecting revenue on which the very life of the state depends, the courts do not always scrutinize captiously the incidental regulative effects of taxes. This is seen in their permissive attitude towards a protective tariff which evidently is not a tax for revenue but a tax for the transfer of values from one class to another class. This is what the police power does in its guise of control over foreign commerce by the protective tariff.

For the police power is none other than the sovereign power to restrain or suppress what is deemed, by the dominant interests, to be disadvantageous, and to promote and foster what they deem advantageous for the commonwealth. Taxation then, is the most pervasive and privileged exercise of the police power. . . . Even when not consciously intended to be regulative, taxes nevertheless regulate, for they, like the protective tariff, determine the directions in which people may become wealthy by determining directions in which they may not become wealthy. They say to the business man: Here is profit, there is loss. It is impossible to avoid these effects of taxes, therefore impossible to escape the police power of taxation, therefore impossible to look upon taxes of any kind whatever as merely a means of obtaining revenue according to any principle of equality, or ability to pay, or accumulation of wealth, or any standard that looks solely to the acquisitions of the past. Taxation is, in fact, a process of obtaining public revenue by proportioning inducements to obtain profits. It always has these effects, and, in fact, all legislators and assessors actually do consider the expected effects. However, it is but doing openly, what taxing authorities are already doing privately or blindly, even corruptly. . . .[17]

The use of the term *police power of taxation* makes explicit this otherwise hardly acknowledged aspect of the government's general power of taxation. The prospective nature of "proportioning inducements" is the instrument that is of particular interest to us in the development of land-planning policy.

Notes

1. In Seligman, *Essays in Taxation, supra* chapter 2, note 28, at chapter XIV therein.

2. Expropriation may but ordinarily does not result in revenue.

3. While Professor Seligman does not mention the criminal law doctrine of *scienter* here in his discussion, it is without doubt an important additional reason for such a distinction.

4. See *Robinson v. California*, 370 U.S. 660 (1962).

5. Seligman, *supra* chapter 2, note 28, at 402.

6. Cooley, *Taxation* (2d ed., 1886) at 587.

7. These and other related cases are treated in more detail in chapter 4.

8. Cf. *City of N.Y. v. Second Ave. R.R. Co.*, 32 N.Y. 261 (1865) (tax held void), with *Frankford & Phila. Pass. Rwy. v. Philadelphia*, 58 Pa. 119 (1868) (tax held valid). What was held "reasonable" in one case was declared "unreasonable" in the other.

9. *Burch v. Savannah*, 42 Ga. 596 (1870).

10. *Youngblood v. Sexton*, 32 Mich. 406 (1875).

11. Seligman, *supra* chapter 2, note 28, at 404.

12. *Id.* at 406.

13. For instance, in assessing benefits the assessors cannot restrict themselves to the cost of the improvement in front of a particular lot. *Ex Parte Mayor of Albany*, 23 Wend. 277 (1840).

14. Cf. *State v. Newark*, 37 N.J.L. 415 (1874); *Bogert v. Elizabeth*, 27 N.J.Eq. 568 (1876).

15. The presumption of special benefit has been broadly construed. See *Matter of Church*, 92 N.Y. 1 (1883); *Allen v. Drew*, 44 Vt. 174 (1872).

16. See particularly Commons, *Institutional Economics* (1934) (U. of Wisc. Reprint, 1964).

17. *Id.* Vol. 2, at 819-821 (U. of Wisc. Reprint, 1964).

4 Regulatory Powers of Congress Through Taxation: Opinions of the U.S. Supreme Court

Whether or not, and to what extent, Congress can regulate through the use of the power of taxation is a question that has been dealt with in a broad line of cases that have come to the U.S. Supreme Court over the years. The opinions cover a wide array of subjects that are not, for the most part, related to taxes that affect land. However, they are sufficiently comparable in the exercise of government authority to be fairly determinative on this subject, too. These cases will be briefly summarized to obtain a basic profile of the Court's thinking in this area.

Destructive Taxation

In *Veazie Bank v. Fenno,*[1] the Court upheld a 10 percent tax on state bank notes that had been imposed with the obvious (though not express) intention of driving them out of existence and creating a uniform system of national currency. The Court was able to base its holding in this case on the existence of enumerated powers (that is, the power to borrow and to coin money under art. I, § 8, cl. 2 and cl. 5 of the Constitution), and their extension under the "necessary-and-proper" clause, as elaborated by Justice Marshall in *McCulloch v. Maryland.*[2]

In *McCray v. U.S.,*[3] a federal excise tax of ten cents a pound, imposed on yellow-colored margarine, as opposed to a tax of one-quarter of a cent a pound on white (uncolored) margarine, clearly aimed at discouraging its use as a butter substitute, was upheld by the Court. It here chose to sustain the tax as a revenue measure on its face, not seeking to justify it on the basis of any other enumerated power, nor attempting to look behind the statute to its legislative history to discover regulatory intent. The Court stated: "The remedy lies, not in the abuse of the judicial authority of its functions, but in the people . . . the motive or purpose of Congress in adopting the acts in question may not be inquired into . . . on their face they levy an excise tax. That being their necessary scope and operation, it follows that the acts are within the grant of power [of the Constitution] . . . if a tax be within the lawful power, the exertion of that power may not be judicially restrained because of the results to arise from its exercise. . . ."

It is interesting to note that the Court dismissed Fifth Amendment due process and Tenth Amendment reserved-power considerations by noting that ". . . nothing in those amendments operates to take away the grant of power to tax conferred by the Constitution upon Congress. The contention on this subject rests upon the theory that the purpose and motive of Congress in exercising its undoubted powers may be inquired into by the courts, and the proposition is therefore disposed of by what has been said on that subject."

Regarding the general question of destruction through taxation, the Court noted that the government may prohibit the manufacture of margarine *outright* without the violation of fundamental rights.[4]

In *Felsenheld v. U.S.*,[5] the Court upheld the provisions of a federal taxing act prohibiting the inclusion in packages of tobacco or cigarettes anything but tobacco products, including premium coupons, in order to protect the integrity of the objects of the excise tax.

In *Sonzinski v. U.S.*,[6] an annual license tax on dealers in firearms was upheld although limited to persons dealing in sawed-off shotguns and rifles, machine guns, and silencers, devices particularly related to criminal activity the federal government intended to control. Again, the Court was able to read the Act as a revenue measure only on its face, ignoring its legislative history: "We are not free to speculate as to the motives which moved Congress to impose it."

In *U.S. v. Doremus*,[7] a special tax was imposed under the Harrison Narcotic Drug Act of 1914 on the manufacture, importation, and sale or gift of opium or coca leaves or their compounds. The supervision, inspection, collection, and enforcement provisions of the Act were held not to violate the state's reserved powers under the Tenth Amendment but were sufficiently related to facilitating the collection of an otherwise valid federal excise tax so as to be within the scope of the necessary-and-proper clause.

In *Nigro v. U.S.*,[8] again upholding the Narcotic Drug Act under review in the *Doremus* case, *supra*, the Court was quick to point to the fact that Congress had since increased the tax rate from a nominal to a substantial one, as proof that the Act was not a subterfuge for a regulatory scheme!

In *U.S. v. Sanchez*,[9] the Court upheld a registration requirement and also the use of official order blanks for the purchase of marihuana, with a tax to be paid at the rate of one dollar per ounce for those not so registered under the provisions of the Marihuana Tax Act.[10] The House and Senate Reports on the original Bills contained clear statements of regulatory purpose.[11] The Court pointed out: "It is beyond serious question that a tax does not cease to be valid merely because it regulates, discourages, or even definitely deters the activities taxed." It then added: "Nor does a tax statute necessarily fail because it touches on activities which Congress might not otherwise regulate."[12] This remark by Mr. Justice Clark is one that is worthy of the most careful attention with regard to the scope of the federal legislative power.

In *U.S. v. Kahriger*,[13] the Court upheld the provisions of the Revenue Act of 1951, imposing a 10 percent tax on wagers not licensed by the state and requiring the purchase of a fifty-dollar occupational stamp tax by those receiving wagers. The Act also required registration of names, addresses, and places of business; this was sanctioned by the Court as being directly related to the collection of the tax. The Court observed further: ". . . that a federal excise tax does not cease to be valid merely because it discourages or deters the activities taxed. Nor is the tax invalid because the revenue obtained is negligible." While the Court dismissed the issue of self-incrimination under the Fifth Amendment here, it was subsequently successfully interjected in *Marchetti v. U.S.*[14] and *Grosso v. U.S.*[15]

A similar result was reached in *Haynes v. U.S.*,[16] with regard to the registration requirements of the National Firearms Act of 1934, and in *Leary v. U.S.*,[17] with regard to the Marihuana Tax Act of 1954. But the Fifth Amendment restrictions of the power to regulate these subjects have now been substantially obviated by *U.S. v. Freed*,[18] holding that amendments to the law providing for procedural exclusions of evidence could successfully avoid the objections relating to self-incrimination.

It is perhaps important to note here that the Court has seen fit to distinguish "an essentially non-criminal area of inquiry" from that of the foregoing cases, where registration, filing of forms, and recordkeeping may reasonably be required.[19]

Welfare, Commerce, and Reserved Powers

In *Bailey v. Drexel Furniture Co.*,[20] "The Child Labor Tax Case," a 10 percent tax on net profits imposed under the Child Labor Tax Law[21] for employing a child under the specified minimum age was held invalid as a penalty and regulation of an area reserved to the states by the Tenth Amendment. The Court depended heavily on *Hammer v. Dagenhart*,[22] which held invalid the Keating-Owens (Child Labor) Act of 1916,[23] prohibiting the shipment of goods in interstate commerce where children under the minimum age had been employed. This earlier case represented a restrictive view of the powers delegated to Congress by the commerce clause (art. I, § 8, cl. 3), and has since been overruled by *U.S. v. Darby*,[24] where the Court upheld the Fair Labor Standards Act of 1938.[25] The *Darby* case, however, did not appear to directly address the *Bailey* decision, leaving open to question regulation under the taxing power alone, as opposed to (or unsupported by) other enumerated powers.[26]

While it can be seen that judicial exploration of congressional intent has for the most part been avoided in reviewing taxation matters, in *U.S. v. Constantine*,[27] the Court did set aside a special excise tax of $1,000, imposed on liquor dealers operating in violation of state or municipal law, as opposed to a nominal tax on those complying with the local law, after repeal of the Eighteenth Amendment ("Prohibition"), as an "invasion of the police power inherent in the States." Justice Cardozo, in his dissent, referred to this approach as an attempt to "psychoanalyze" Congress. It is not thought that the Court would now be inclined to continue with such approach.[28]

Taxing and Spending as Independent Powers

The case of *U.S. v. Butler*[29] is also of special significance here. Under the Agricultural Adjustment Act of 1933,[30] a tax on the processing of agricultural products for the purposes of crop reduction and price raising was held to be unconstitutional. Although firmly maintaining that the taxing and spending power *for the general welfare* under art. I., § 8, cl. 1, was to be considered an independent enumerated power of Congress (and it was chosen to decide the case on this narrow issue), the Court nevertheless concluded that the Act of 1933 invaded the reserve powers of the states under the Tenth Amendment. This conclusion was clearly based, of course, on the assumption followed in the *Bailey* case, and *Hammer v. Dagenhart, supra*, before it, that "production" was a subject matter intended to be wholly reserved to the states.[31]

Justices Stone, Cardozo and Brandeis in their dissent in the *Butler* case were quick to pick up the patent inconsistency of holding, on the one hand, that taxing and spending for the general welfare was a separate ("enumerated") congressional power and, on the other, that the reserved powers of the states had been violated by the imposition of conditions by Congress relating to the purpose of the expenditure. Although there is no really satisfactory way to reconcile the obvious contradiction involved in the majority's reasoning, we see here a distinction attempted, as in many other cases, between: (1) taxing to raise money *to spend*, for either (a) the general welfare or (b) the subject area of an enumerated power; and (2) the power to *regulate* through taxation where an enumerated power *other than* taxing *and* spending for the general welfare will be required.[32] Apparently, the fear of further expansion of the welfare clause is responsible for the continued viability of such distinctions.[33]

Of course, it must be recognized that the concurrent state and federal power of taxation, already touched upon, can be a special complicating factor in these issues.[34]

The correlative importance of the spending power as an independent power delegated to Congress is apparent in *Helvering v. Davis*,[35] where the validity of the old-age-assistance provisions of the Social Security Act were upheld, and in *Stewart Machine Co. v. Davis*,[36] decided earlier that same day, upholding a federal program of assistance for unemployment relief under the same Act.[37]

Apparently, the fact that the objectives sought to be carried out by the spending power could not have been achieved by direct regulation, due to the absence of an enumerated power on the subject to sustain it, does not necessarily make a taxing program invalid.[38]

The Question of a "Federal Police Power"

Any discussion of the federal power of taxation as a regulatory device inevitably leads to a broader realm of speculation as to the existence of a "federal police power." To the extent that such a power exists, it is seen as being derived from the expansion of several enumerated powers,[39] but principally from the commerce clause, on the one hand, and the taxing clause, on the other, as extended in each case by the necessary-and-proper clause to the broader dimensions already indicated. It is clear enough that the widest regulatory powers that relate to the classic "public health, safety, morals and general welfare" were intended to be reserved fairly exclusively to the States.[40] It has also been seen that insofar as the subject of "general welfare" would be concerned, it is only with regard to *conditioned spending* of tax revenues that federal regulatory powers were openly conceded by the Court.

The Doctrine of "Resultant" Powers

At this point it is important to consider the significance of another Hamiltonian doctrine, also taken up and espoused by Justice Story in his *Commentaries*,[41] that viewed the enumerated powers as not mutually exclusive but capable of being combined, and thus creating so-called "resultant" powers. The inherent implications of this doctrine for regulatory purposes can hardly be ignored. The doctrine was forcefully expressed in *The Legal Tender Cases*: ". . . it is not indispensable to the existence of any power claimed for the federal government that it can be found specified in the words of the Constitution, or clearly and directly traceable to some one of the specified powers. Its existences may be deduced fairly from more than one of the substantive powers expressly defined, or from them all combined. It is allowable to group together any number of them and infer from them all that the power claimed has been conferred. Such a treatment of the Constitution is recognized by its own provisions."[42] A number of cases have elaborated upon this view,[43] which can be traced, perhaps somewhat ironically, to Justice Marshall's efforts to expound the doctrine of enumerated powers in *McCulloch v. Maryland*.[44]

Standing to Sue

A final comment should be made at this time regarding the reluctance of the Court to recognize legal standing to contest the validity of federal appropriations.[45] What first appeared to be a strong refusal to find such standing has now been substantially modified; however, a more careful reading of the Court's new criteria indicates that regulatory, as opposed to spending, measures would be still more difficult, if not impossible, to attack as a general taxpayer.[46]

Notes

1. 8 Wall. 533 (1869). While this case is generally treated as the landmark on the subject, it is interesting to consider that the measures imposed on distilled spirits and ("pleasure") carriages by the Act of March 3, 1791, and later the Act of June 5, 1794, 1 Stat. 373, ch. 45, upheld as to the latter in *Hylton v. U.S.*, *supra* chapter 2, note 17, were proposed by Alexander Hamilton and intended, "more as a measure of social discipline than as a source of revenue." See 1 Morison, *Oxford History of the United States* 182 (1927). The *Hylton* case was thus also the first case before the U.S. Supreme Court where the validity of the exercise of the taxing power was considered.

2. *Supra* chapter 2, note 1. The case is further discussed *infra* pp. 31, 39 and 40; notes 24 and 44 this chapter; chapter 5, note 4.

3. 195 U.S. 27 (1904). See also, *In re Kollock*, 165 U.S. 526 (1897), where regulations concerning packaging and labeling margarine ostensibly to prevent fraud in the collection of the tax were upheld.

4. While no citation is referred to in Justice White's opinion, it most probably alludes to the holding in *Powell v. Pennsylvania*, 127 U.S. 678 (1888), where outright prohibition on margarine sales by state law was upheld. The extension to the federal government of this reasoning gives the case a perhaps unintentionally enhanced police-power flavor. Cf. *Schollenberger v. Pennsylvania*, 171 U.S. 1 (1898), holding prohibition on interstate sales invalid.

5. 186 U.S. 126 (1902).

6. 300 U.S. 506 (1937).

7. 249 U.S. 86 (1919).

8. 276 U.S. 332 (1928). See also *Alston v. U.S.*, 274 U.S. 289 (1927).

9. 340 U.S. 42 (1950).

10. Act of August 2, 1937, ch. 553, 50 Stat. 551.

11. S. Rep. No. 900, 75th Cong., 1st Sess. 3; H.R. Rep. No. 792, 75th Cong., 1st Sess. 2.

12. 340 U.S. at 44.

13. 345 U.S. 22 (1953). See also, *Lewis v. U.S.*, 348 U.S. 419 (1955). (Violation of gambling tax act in District of Columbia).

14. 390 U.S. 39 (1968).

15. 390 U.S. 62 (1968). See also, *Mackey v. U.S.*, 401 U.S. 667 (1971).

16. 390 U.S. 85 (1968).

17. 395 U.S. 6 (1969).

18. 401 U.S. 601 (1971). Thus, *Kahringer, Lewis, Doremus*, and *Sonzinsky* were ostensibly overruled only *pro tanto*.

19. See *U.S. v. Sullivan*, 274 U.S. 259 (1927), permitting such requirements for income tax collection purposes, and *Shapiro v. U.S.*, 335 U.S. 1 (1948), for the administration of the Emergency Price Control Act of 1942. See also Corwin, *supra* chapter 2, note 31, at 382, for a discussion of the so-called "required-records doctrine."

20. 259 U.S. 20 (1922).

21. Act of February 24, 1919, title XII, 40 Stat. 1138.

22. 247 U.S. 251 (1918).

23. Act of September 1, 1916, 39 Stat. 675. After being disappointed by the decision on this Act by the Supreme Court, the opponents of child labor sought to apply the thinking of the *McCray* case in furtherance of their cause by immediately recasting the regulatory scheme to take the form of a taxing act. Their haste in attending to the draftsmanship appears to have been particularly ill-advised, for it is not unlikely that the Court was left with some anxiety about the future uses of the taxing power. Neither *Bailey* nor *McCray* have ever been overruled by the Court. Technically speaking, they are distinguishable simply on the basis of the latter being "but a revenue measure on its face" and the former unfortunately, being more outspoken.

24. 312 U.S. 100 (1941). A resurrection of the issues in the case of *McCulloch v. Maryland, supra* chapter 2, note 1, is here observable. In that case, Justice Marshall, in holding that the national government could incorporate its own bank, although not expressly empowered to do so, promoted the expansion of the congressional enumerated powers through the use of the necessary-and-proper clause. He there pointed out that the word *expressly*, used with regard to the powers to be delegated to the United States in the Articles of Confederation, was not carried over into the U.S. Constitution. However, *Hammer v. Dagenhart, supra* note 22, attempted to carry it over by judicial interpretation in 1918. The *Darby* case, therefore, effectively reasserted Marshall's position with regard to the extent of the commerce-clause powers of Congress, which was more specifically elaborated by him in the case of *Gibbons v. Ogden, supra* chapter 2, note 40. The Court's initial reluctance to permit Congress to exercise regulatory (police) powers in this way over the subject matter of employment and production, attempting to except them from the meaning of the words "commerce . . . among the several States," is of important comparative significance to the power of tax-

ation. See also *N.L.R.B. v. Jones & Laughlin Steel Co.*, 301 U.S. 1 (1937), upholding the National Labor Relations Act.

25. 52 Stat. 1060, ch. 676.

26. See *Hill v. Wallace*, 259 U.S. 44 (1922), and *Trusler v. Crooks*, 269 U.S. 475 (1926), holding invalid a grain futures tax on those not complying with regulations promulgated by the Secretary of Agriculture under the Futures Trading Act of 1921; *Board of Trade of Chicago v. Olsen*, 262 U.S. 1 (1923), upholding the Grain Futures Trading Act of 1922 as a permissible regulation of interstate commerce; *Carter v. Carter Coal Co.*, 298 U.S. 238 (1936), holding invalid a tax on coal subject to 90 percent credits for those submitting to pricing, labor, and trade-practices regulations (applying the old "movement" definition of interstate commerce); and *Sunshine Anthracite Coal Co. v. Adkins*, 310 U.S. 381 (1940), upholding exemptions from a 19.5 percent tax on sales of coal in interstate commerce to those submitting themselves to regulation of prices and competition. The Court here stated: "Clearly this tax is not designed merely for revenue purposes. In purpose and effect it is primarily a sanction to enforce the regulatory provisions of the Act. But that does not mean that the statute is invalid and the tax unenforceable. Congress may impose penalties in aid of the exercise of any of its enumerated powers. The power of taxation, granted to Congress by the Constitution, may be utilized as a sanction for the exercise of another power which is granted to it." See also *Railroad Retirement Board v. Alton R.R. Co.*, 295 U.S. 330 (1935), holding invalid the taxing provisions of the Railroad Retirement Act, later amended and then upheld in *California v. Anglim*, 129 F2d 455 (CCA 9th, 1942) cert. den. 317 U.S. 669 (1942).

27. 296 U.S. 287 (1935).

28. Corwin, *supra* chapter 2, note 31, at 42.

29. 297 U.S. 1 (1936), the "1st A.A.A. Case."

30. Act of May 12, 1933, ch. 25, 48 Stat. 31.

31. As indicated, this interpretation of the Tenth Amendment was soon to be abandoned in the *Darby* case. After *Butler*, the Court moved on to sustain similar measures under the now less-restricted view of the commerce clause. See *Mulford v. Smith*, 307 U.S. 38 (1939), sustaining penalties of one-half the market price of all tobacco sold above a quota under the Agricultural Adjustment Act of February 16, 1938, 52 Stat. 45, the "2nd A.A.A. Case." See also *Wickard v. Filburn*, 317 U.S. 111 (1942), where any of the remaining pretenses preserved by the *Mulford* case were completely cast aside, upholding penalties for violation of production quotas on wheat grown by the defendant for consumption by himself and his stock, since this would have "a substantial influence" on price and market conditions: ". . . it supplies the need of the man who grew it which would otherwise be reflected by purchases in the open market. . . . Questions of the power of Congress are not to be decided by reference to any formula which

would give controlling force to nomenclature such as 'production''' (construing the Agricultural Adjustment Act of 1938, as amended by the Act of 1941, 52 Stat. 31).

This move, in fact, was long ago anticipated in the *Head Money Cases*, 112 U.S. 580 (1884), where a tax on ship owners for each alien passenger was sustained as ''. . . not . . . strictly speaking a tax or duty within the meaning of the Constitution,'' but a regulation of (foreign) commerce.

It should be carefully noted, however, that the *Butler* case has not been overruled with regard to its position on the taxing-spending power as an independent source of authority for Congress, when read together with the "welfare" clause. It is, perhaps surprisingly, treated as authoritative on that point, representing the original so-called "Hamilton," as opposed to "Madison" view of the welfare clause. See Corwin, *supra* chapter 2, note 31, at 43. See also 36 Harv. L. Rev. 548-582 (1923). The Hamilton view was further elaborated by Justice Story in his work, *Commentaries on the Constitution of the United States* (5th ed.), vol. I, ch. XIV, and heavily depended upon by the Court in its decision.

32. In addition, to be sure, the "blindfold test" of the *McCray* case would continue to be preserved, where an "otherwise valid tax on its face" is involved. See also *U.S. v. Sanchez, supra* note 9.

33. See Corwin, *supra* chapter 2, note 31, at 44-45.

34. The effect of the "supremacy" clause, art. VI, cl. 2, of the Constitution, must be taken into account here as being somewhat different from its effect where other enumerated powers are concerned. See chapter 5 herein. See also *supra* chapter 2, note 40.

35. 301 U.S. 619 (1937).

36. *Supra* chapter 2, note 31. The unemployment provisions of the Social Security Act provided for a federal payroll tax on employers, with the proviso that if a state had adopted an acceptable compensation plan according to federal guidelines, the employer could credit up to 90 percent of his payments to the state program against his federal payroll tax. No state could realistically ignore the economic and political implications of not setting up such a program, especially since the federal government was not providing an alternative program of its own. Amounts paid to the United States were to go into general funds in the Treasury. Also, a grant-in-aid provision permitted state administrative costs to be defrayed by the federal government, appropriated out of unearmarked Treasury funds. The Court was able to point to contractual agreements with the states, as well as nonearmarking of revenues, as attributes not present in the *Butler* case. That the latter distinction proves to be less convincing than the former, see *Cincinnati Soap Co. v. U.S.*, 301 U.S. 308 (1937).

It will also be recalled that a successful use of a similar tax-credit incentive had been made in *Florida v. Mellon, supra* chapter 2, note 10, where inheritance taxes were concerned, without violating the rule of uniformity.

37. Act of August 14, 1935, 49 Stat. 620.

38. In upholding the unemployment-relief provisions, the Court hedged on this question by stating: "In ruling as we do, we leave many questions open. We do not say that a tax is valid, when imposed by act of Congress, if it is laid upon the condition that a state may escape its operation through the adoption of a statute unrelated in subject matter to the activities fairly within the scope of national policy and power." 301 U.S. at 590.

It is also worth considering in this context the statement in the case of *Magnano Co. v. Hamilton*, 292 U.S. 40 (1934), another tax measure involving margarine: "From the beginning of our government, the courts have sustained taxes although imposed with the collateral intent of effecting ulterior ends which, considered apart, were beyond the constitutional power of the lawmakers to realize by legislation directly addressed to their accomplishments." Although a state regulation was involved here, it is important to realize that the case was cited in the *Sanchez* case, *supra* p. 28 in support of a broad exercise of federal power, much in the same way that the *McCray* case, *supra* pp. 27-28 and notes 3 and 4, referred to "outright" prohibition of margarine manufacture.

39. For a development of the sources of such power, see the early definitive articles written on the subject by Robert E. Cushman: *Commerce Power*, 3 Minn.L.Rev. 289, 381, 452 (1919); *Taxation*, 4 Minn.L.Rev. 247 (1920), 18 Minn.L.Rev. 759 (1934); *Postal Power*, 4 Minn.L.Rev. 402 (1920).

40. See *The License Cases, supra* chapter 2, note 35, where the police power was most concisely defined as "the power to govern men and things." See also *Charles River Bridge Co. v. Warren Bridge*, 11 Pet. 420, 547-548 (1837).

41. 2 Story, *Commentaries on the Constitution of the United States*, §§ 1256, 1286, and 1330 (1833).

42. 12 Wall. 457 (1871).

43. *Juilliard v. Greenman*, 110 U.S. 421 (1884) (legal tender); *U.S. v. Gettysburg Electric Rwy.*, 160 U.S. 668 (1896) (here the Court invoked "the great power of taxation to be exercised for the common defence and general welfare" in support of the right of the federal government to acquire by eminent domain land for use as a national park); *City of Cleveland v. U.S.*, 323 U.S. 329 (1945) (eminent domain).

44. *Supra* chapter 2, note 1. The idea is more fully elaborated by Marshall in *American Insurance Co. v. Canter*, 1 Pet. 511, (1828), with relation to admiralty jurisdiction.

45. *Massachusetts v. Mellon* and *Frothingham v. Mellon*, 262 U.S. 447 (1923). Both the state and the taxpayer were denied standing to restrain disbursements of federal money in a program to reduce maternal and infant mortality.

46. In *Flast v. Cohen*, 392 U.S. 83 (1968), taxpayers were found to have standing to contest the expenditure of federal moneys to assist religious-affiliated educational organizations. Justice Warren here asserted that the question of standing depends upon whether there is "a logical nexus between the status asserted and the claim sought to be adjudicated. . . . The nexus demanded of federal taxpayers has two aspects to it. First, the taxpayer must establish a logical link between that status and the type of legislative enactment attacked. Thus, a taxpayer will be a proper party to allege the unconstitutionality only of exercises of congressional power under the taxing and spending clause of Art. I, § 8, of the Constitution. It will not be sufficient to allege an incidental expenditure of tax funds in the administration of an essentially regulatory statute. . . . Secondly, the taxpayer must establish a nexus between that status and the precise nature of the constitutional infringement alleged. Under this requirement, the taxpayer must show that the challenged enactment exceeds specific constitutional limitations imposed upon the exercise of the congressional taxing and spending power and not simply that the enactment is generally beyond the powers delegated to Congress by Art. I, §8." *Frothingham* and *Flast* both can meet the first test since they attacked a spending program rather than a regulatory scheme. *Flast* met the second test because of the First Amendment "establishment" clause, "which operates as a specific constitutional limitation upon the exercise in Congress of the taxing and spending power. . . ." The Tenth Amendment thus was not a sufficient basis in the *Frothingham* case. "Whether the Constitution contains other specific limitations can only be determined in the context of future cases." 392 U.S. at 102-105.

5

Regulatory Powers of the States and Their Instrumentalities Through Taxation: Further Opinions of the U.S. Supreme Court

So far the concern has been with regulatory powers of Congress through taxation. There are also important federal constitutional limitations on both the state's power of taxation and the state's police power as such. These also will now be generally reviewed by reference to decisions of the U.S. Supreme Court.

Heritage of the *McCulloch* Case

In *McCulloch v. Maryland*, already discussed,[1] the companion issue to that of the national government's power to incorporate a bank was the state's power to tax its bank notes if it did not comply with the requirements of the state's banking laws. The decision holding such action invalid effectively established the Court's position on the question of federal supremacy, under art. VI, cl. 2, of the Constitution.[2] This had the interesting effect of supporting later decisions placing lands owned by the federal government *itself* beyond the reach of taxation by the states,[3] yet, in distinction, regarding the federally chartered institution in the *McCulloch* case, the Court stated: "This opinion does not deprive the States of any resources which they originally possessed. It does not extend to a tax paid by the real property[4] of the bank, in common with the other real property within the State, nor to a tax imposed on the interest which the citizens of Maryland may hold in this institution, in common with other property of the same description throughout the State. But this is a tax on the operations of the bank, and is, consequently, a tax on the operation of an instrument employed by the government of the Union to carry its powers into execution. Such a tax must be unconstitutional."[5] Inherent in this statement are three significant sets of distinctions: (1) between the federal government itself and something that is its instrument (here, a corporate entity it had created); (2) between real estate and the "operations" that may take place thereon (that is, land use); and (3) between a tax for revenue (here, essentially what we would refer to as an ad valorem tax on realty) and taxation for regulatory purposes (in this case, destructive). Thus, at an early stage, these important theoretical considerations were both readily observed and enunciated.

Perhaps it would now be worthwhile to trace this initial elaboration by the Court of the supremacy clause over the succeeding years, in order to understand better its effect upon the subject of our study.

Immunity or Exemption of Government Agents, Instrumentalities, and Contractors

In *Osborn v. United States Bank*,[6] the State of Ohio had defied the decision of the Court in the *McCulloch* case and had attempted to collect a similar tax from the United States Bank. In an attempt to press in its favor the distinction recognized in *McCulloch* between "instruments" of the federal government and the government itself (e.g., the U.S. Mint)—analogizing the former to contractors—the state found that it had given Justice Marshall the opportunity to rule that even contractors, together with other instruments, were to be considered within the meaning of the supremacy clause.

For well over a century thereafter, there was an extensive expansion to all sorts of activities and instrumentalities of the doctrine of governmental immunity from taxation, including the development of a parallel thesis on the part of the states—that there were, in fact, two inviolate sovereignties, as if there were two supremacy clauses operating simultaneously in two exclusive spheres of influence (the Tenth Amendment serving the states in that capacity).[7]

In *Collector v. Day*, discussed *supra* page 8, the idea of mutual immunity of government officials and other instruments was not considered inconsistent with the *McCulloch* decision. However, the practical necessities of financing for both levels of government in the years to come were no doubt ultimately responsible for the repudiation of the concept.

In *Graves v. New York ex rel. O'Keefe*, Justice Stone stated: "The burden, so far as it can be said to exist or to affect the government in any indirect or incidental way, is one which the Constitution presupposes; and hence it cannot rightly be deemed to be within an implied restriction upon the taxing power of the national and state governments which the Constitution has expressly granted to one and has confirmed to the other. The immunity is not one to be implied from the Constitution, because if allowed it would impose to an inadmissible extent a restriction on the taxing power which the Constitution has reserved to the state governments."[8]

Thus, *Collector v. Day, New York ex rel. Rogers v. Graves*,[9] and *Dobbins v. Erie County*[10] were ". . . overruled so far as they recognize an implied constitutional immunity from income taxation of the salaries of officers or employees of the national or a State government or their instrumentalities." Just prior to this ruling in *Collector v. Day*, the Court had already laid the groundwork for its new position with regard to government contractors in *James v. Dravo Contracting Co.*,[11] where it had held that a state may impose an occupation tax upon an independent contractor, measured by gross receipts under contracts with the United States.

Of the many cases considering the activities of contractors, perhaps the most significant one for our concern with land is *Wilson v. Cook*,[12] where a severance tax on a contractor severing and purchasing timber from federally owned lands was upheld by the Court. Other cases of importance in this area are: *Alabama v. King & Boozer*,[13] upholding a state sales tax on building materials purchased and used by a building contractor in the performance of a cost-plus-fixed-fee contract with the United States to build army camps, with title to the materials passing to the federal government; *Superior Bath House Co. v. McCarroll*[14] and *Buckstaff Bath House v. McKinley*,[15] where income and social security taxes, respectively, were upheld on the operators of bath houses under lease from the federal government in the National Park System. Similarly, property taxes may be levied against land under water owned by a person holding a license under the Federal Water Power Act;[16] and land conveyed by the federal government to a corporation for dry-dock purposes was subject to general property taxes, despite a reservation in the conveyance of rights to free usage of the dock and provisions for forfeiture in the event of discontinuation of, or unfitness for, the use specified.[17]

Federally chartered fiscal institutions or finance agencies remain subject to taxation only with the consent of Congress, and only in conformity with the restrictions it has attached to its consent.[18] In *Baltimore National Bank v. Tax Comm.*[19] and *Maricopa County v. Valley Bank*,[20] the Court construed statutes first allowing then exempting from taxation shares of the Reconstruction Finance Corporation. In *Pittman v. Home Owners Loan Corp.*,[21] a state tax on mortgages securing a loan by the Home Owners Loan Corporation was held invalid, but here the federal act creating the corporation also provided for exemption from state and municipal taxes. In *Federal Land Bank of St. Paul v. Bismark Lumber Co.*,[22] the bank was held exempt from a state sales tax as applied to materials used for improvement of farm property acquired by the bank as a result of foreclosure proceedings, although this might be considered a "proprietary" function; here, too, exemption was provided for, in this case by the Federal Farm Loan Act of 1916. Similarly, a lease by a federal land bank of oil and gas in a mineral estate, which it had reserved in land originally acquired through foreclosure and had then conveyed to a third party, was held immune from a state tax levied on the lease and the royalties therefrom.[23]

In the case of *Carson v. Roane-Anderson Co.*,[24] the Court held that, under the Atomic Energy Act of 1946, all property, income, and activities of the Atomic Energy Commission and its contractors were free from all state and local taxes, reflecting a full assertion of the supremacy and necessary-and-proper clauses.

After a long period of applying the immunity doctrine to lessees of Indian lands, the Court here, too, withdrew exemptions unless affirmatively granted by Congress, and in the case of *Oklahoma Tax Comm. v. Texas Co.*[25] held that the lessee of mineral rights in restricted Indian lands was subject to gross production and excise taxes, unless expressly exempted by Congressional action.

Federal "Enclaves"

Another special constitutional provision, relating to what are termed *federal enclaves*, is found in art. I, §8, cl. 17, giving Congress the power "To exercise exclusive Legislation in all Cases whatsoever, over such District (not exceeding ten Miles square) as may, by Cession of Particular States, and the Acceptance of Congress, become the Seat of the Government of the United States, and to exercise like Authority over all Places purchased by the Consent of the Legislature of the State in which the Same shall be, for the Erection of Forts, Magazines, Arsenals, dock-Yards and other needful Buildings. . . ." This provision applies not only to the District of Columbia, but to all "Places" and "other needful Buildings" acquired by the federal government.[26] Thus, in *Humble Pipe Line Co. v. Waggonner*,[27] oil and gas leases to private parties on a federal Air Force base were exempt from ad valorem taxation, notwithstanding the following facts: (1) that the land was donated by the State of Louisiana to the federal government (not purchased); (2) that the leases were made through the Department of Interior, rather than the Air Force; and (3) that a contractual agreement was made that the lessee pay all federal and state taxes.[28] The Court held that a standard agreement to pay all taxes did not operate as an abandonment of exclusive federal jurisdiction, nor did payment of the state school system per capita charges by the federal government constitute a rejection of such jurisdiction. It pointed out that when Congress has wished to allow a state to exercise jurisdiction to levy certain taxes within a federal enclave, it has specifically so stated (e.g., the Buck Act, 4 U.S.C., §§104-111).

It is to be carefully noted that art. I, §8, cl. 17, requires that there be consent of the state legislature in order to vest "exclusive" power in Congress. Many of the states have now adopted general statutes consenting in advance to the acquisition of property by the federal government. Yet even here jurisdiction does not pass unless Congress accepts it.[29] Moreover, it was once considered that a state's surrender of jurisdiction to the federal government under art. I, §8, cl. 17, had to be substantially unqualified. However, in *James v. Dravo Contracting Co.*,[30] the Court held that it was valid for a state to convey and the United States to accept "concurrent" jurisdiction and authority over such land, "as is not inconsistent with the jurisdiction ceded to the United States." The effect of the decisions cited relating to permissible conditions that a state may attach to property ceded to the federal government under this clause has resulted in altering the literal meaning of exclusive jurisdiction. Thus, on the basis of such authority, a state may readily reserve the power of taxation as a condition of ceding to the federal government.[31]

Other Questions of Federal Interest

In *Rohr Aircraft Corp. v. San Diego County*,[32] real property owned by the Reconstruction Finance Corporation and specifically subjected to local taxation by the Reconstruction Finance Act, under the then-existing policy of waiver of exemption for financial institutions of this kind, later acquired immunity under the Surplus Property Act of 1944 upon a declaration of surplus under the terms of the latter Act. In spite of the fact that legal title remained in the name of the Reconstruction Finance Corporation, by being given managerial and disposition powers under the Act, the War Assets Administration, when it took possession, acquired "practical ownership" of the property, making it exempt from an ad valorem tax assessment. Pertinent to this holding was the existence, in addition, of a statutory definition of ownership as "custody and control."

However, in *S.R.A., Inc. v. Minnesota*,[33] the Court held that federal retention of a mortgage interest in a former post office under contract of sale for disposal as surplus to the State of Minnesota did not affect relinquishment of exclusive federal jurisdiction and subjected the land and building to taxation at full value at the time of the sale.

Similarly, it was held that where equitable title has passed to the purchaser of land from the federal government, a state may tax the equitable owner on the full value thereof, although legal title has been retained by the federal government;[34] in the case of reclamation entries, taxes may not be collected until equitable title passes.[35]

Discriminatory Taxation

In circumstances where there is a federal "presence," but where governmental immunity would not ordinarily be asserted, there is yet another constraint upon the state taxing power, which is to be found in a judicially developed rule prohibiting discrimination against the federal government; it is not, as might appear at first glance, derived from equal-protection sources, but is seen as one of the incidents of federal supremacy.

Thus, in *Phillips Chemical Co. v. Dumas School Dist.*,[36] where, under state law, a school district does not tax private lessees of state and municipal realty whose leases are subject to termination at the lessor's option in the event of sale, but does levy a tax, measured by the entire value of the realty, on lessees of federal property utilized for private purposes and whose leases are terminable at the option of the United States in an emergency or upon sale, the discrimination voided the tax collected from the federal government. Also, in *Moses Lake Homes v. Grant County*,[37] where privately owned property erected by the lessees on tax-exempt state lands is taxed by a county at less than full value, and houses erected by contractors on land leased from a federal air force base are taxed at full value, the latter tax, solely by reason of the discrimination against the United States and its lessees, is rendered void.

It is interesting, at this point, to go back to the *McCulloch* case to find, among other things, some of the original bases for the development of the rule against tax discrimination by a state where the federal government is concerned.

Regarding state discrimination against nonresidents, see p. 92 and chapter 5, note 71.

Nature of Federal Immunity or Exemption

From what has been said, it may be seen that tax exemption may come into play against the states not only with regard to federally owned land, but where federal activities, uses, or instruments are concerned. More important, private individuals may be but are not necessarily capable of being cloaked with such immunity under certain circumstances. Short of a clear-cut case of outright ownership, the Court has struggled with the development of a workable formula in the effort to balance the revenue/sovereignty/concurrent-power/federal-supremacy issues involved. Along the way, consideration was given to the municipal liability distinction between "proprietary" and "governmental" functions as a test,[38] and to a test to determine whether the tax would be passed on as a cost to the federal government.[39] More recently, it seems to have settled upon a pragmatic "burden" or "interference" test with regard to supremacy or federal sovereignty.[40] The principle of private tax exemption is thus not to be implied directly from the Constitution in these cases, but from an explicit act on the part of Congress to assert such an exemption.[41] It would seem capable of making such an assertion with regard to any case, by virtue of the operation of the necessary-and-proper clause and the supremacy clause in conjunction with one another.[42] Congress would similarly be free to waive such an exemption if it does not involve a breach of contract, and such waivers would generally be liberally construed by the Court in favor of the state or local taxing authority.[43]

State Regulatory Measures

Where the subject of taxation for revenue is concerned, it is easy to see why an attitude of mutual accommodation might readily be encouraged.[44] However, where the power of taxation assumes regulatory character- istics—and therefore may enter other enumerated federal subject areas—the possibility of governmental conflict becomes considerably more likely.[45] From this transitional area we move to sets of cases dealing with outright regulatory efforts by the states (i.e., police-power measures) that have direct pertinence to regulatory tax measures. In approaching this area of potential in- tergovernmental conflict, we are immediately confronted with an extensive vocabulary[46] that has developed in the effort to partition sovereign "ter- ritories" to arrive at a workable accommodation for a dual system of government. There are, in fact, several possibilities: the Court may interpret a given subject area as exclusively within federal jurisdiction under the Con- stitution or may find that affirmative exclusion is necessary by congres- sional action. This, in turn, may be either express or implied, requiring fur- ther interpretation by the Court in the latter event. On the other hand, it may be found that affirmative acceptance of concurrent jurisdiction is necessary. These options are discernible in a number of the cases that follow.

In *Mayo v. U.S.*,[47] a Florida inspection fee on U.S. Department of Agriculture fertilizer distributed in the State under the Soil Conservation Program was held void by the Court as a tax on the exercise of a federal function.

In *Campbell v. Hussey*,[48] a state requirement of identification tags for certain types of tobacco received in warehouses for sale was held invalid by the Court on the grounds that the federal government had occupied the field by enactment of the Tobacco Inspection Act, establishing uniform stan- dards for the classification of tobacco.

In *Florida Lime & Avocado Growers, Inc., v. Paul*,[49] a California statute setting up higher standards for oil content in avocados than the ap- plicable federal standard was upheld by the Court as to Florida produce on the basis that there had been no clear congressional intent to preempt the field. It is interesting to note that the case of *Campbell v. Hussey, supra*, was distinguished on the basis of having attempted to establish uniform standards; here the federal standards were seen as minimum, so that com- pliance with California law would result in compliance with both re- quirements simultaneously.

In *Evansville-Vanderburgh Airport Authority District v. Delta Airlines, Inc.*,[50] a state and municipal user tax of one dollar per passenger emplaning for domestic or interstate flights, for the purpose of defraying the costs of use and maintenance of the airport terminal facilities, was upheld by the

Court on the basis of "fair compensation."[51] However, in *Burbank v. Lockheed Air Terminal*,[52] the Court held invalid city restrictions on the night-time take-off of jet aircraft at a private airport, in view of federal air-traffic regulation by the Federal Aviation Administration and the Environmental Protection Agency under the Noise Control Act of 1972 having effectively preempted the field.

In *Huron Portland Cement Co. v. City of Detroit*,[53] a municipal smoke-abatement ordinance was held by the Court to be enforceable against a ship engaged in interstate commerce in Detroit Harbor using boilers that had been inspected and licensed by the federal government. The Court did point to the lack of proof of multiple or conflicting regulations, and was of the opinion that there was ". . . congressional recognition that the problem of air pollution is peculiarly a matter of state and local concern." To the same effect, in the case of *Kelley v. Washington*,[54] a state law requiring the safety inspection of tug boats was held not to be preempted by the Federal Motorboat Act. Chief Justice Hughes stated: "The principle is thoroughly established, that the exercise by the State of its police power, which would be valid if not superseded by federal action, is superseded only where the repugnance or conflict is so 'direct and positive' that the two acts cannot 'be reconciled or consistently stand together.'"[55] However, where the state goes beyond safety measures only local in their effect and ". . . attempts to impose particular standards . . . which in the judgment of its authorities may be desirable but pass beyond what is plainly essential to safety and seaworthiness, the State will encounter the principle that such requirements, if imposed at all, must be through the action of Congress which can establish a uniform rule. Whether the State in a particular matter goes too far must be left to be determined when the precise question arises."[56]

Related Commerce-Clause Cases

In *Coe v. Errol*,[57] there arose something of a textbook situation with regard to the applicability of the commerce clause to the taxation of timber. Logs cut in Maine had been floated down the Androscoggin River, which flows through New Hampshire on the way to Lewiston, Maine. During the winter, some of these logs were frozen in the river within the town of Errol, New Hampshire. Another collection of logs, cut in New Hampshire, had been taken to the riverbank in Errol to await the thaw for shipment to Maine also. In holding the logs in the latter instance taxable and in the former not, the Court stated: "When the products of the farm or the forest are collected and brought in from the surrounding country to a town or station serving as an entrepôt for that particular region, whether on a river or a line of railroad, such products are not yet exports, nor are they in process of exportation, nor is exportation begun until they are committed to the common carrier for transportation out of the State to the State of their destination, or have started on their ultimate passage to that State. Until then it is reasonable to regard them as not only within the State of their origin, but as a part of the general mass of property of that State, subject to its jurisdiction, and liable to taxation there, if not taxed by reason of their being intended for exportation, but taxed without any discrimination, in the usual way and manner in which such property is taxed in the State. . . . It seems to us untenable to hold that a crop or a herd is exempt from taxation merely because it is, by its owner, intended for exportation. If such were the rule in many States there would be nothing but the lands and real estate to bear the taxes. . . ."

Cases involving minerals and related products of the land are also of interest with regard to the potential effect of the commerce clause:

In *Heisler v. Thomas Colliery Co.*,[58] a Pennsylvania ad valorem tax on anthracite coal, when prepared and ready for shipment, was held not to be an interference with interstate commerce although applied to coal destined for other states.

In *Oliver Iron Co. v. Lord*,[59] an occupation tax on the mining of iron ore was upheld, although most of the ore was immediately loaded on cars and shipped into other states. The Court observed: "Mining is not interstate commerce, but . . . subject to local regulation and taxation. Its character in this regard is intrinsic, is not affected by the intended use or disposal of the product, is not controlled by contractual arrangements, and persists even though the business be conducted in close connection with interstate commerce."

In *Hope Gas Co. v. Hall*,[60] an annual privilege tax on the business of producing natural gas in the state, computed on the value of the gas produced according to gross proceeds from sales, was held constitutional although most of the gas passed into interstate commerce from the wells.

However, in *Eureka Pipe Line Co. v. Hallanan*,[61] oil collected into the pipelines of a distributing company and intended for the most part for customers outside the state was held to be protected by the commerce clause the moment it leaves the wells, and in *United Fuel Gas Co. v. Hallanan*,[62] the same was held to be true with respect to natural gas, so far as taxation is concerned.

In *Pennsylvania Gas Co. v. Public Service Comm.*,[63] however, the Court held that the state may regulate sales in the absence of contrary regulation by Congress.[64]

In an effort to avoid the adverse effects of the commerce clause on state efforts to raise revenue from activities involving interstate commerce, the Commonwealth of Massachusetts devised a method of taxing Western Union, a New York corporation, according to an "apportionment" scheme, taking as a basis such proportion of the value of its capital stock as the length of its lines within the state bore to their entire length throughout the country. In *Western Union Tel. Co. v. Massachusetts*,[65] the Court approved of this method, and it soon had widespread application.[66]

Regulation Based on Police Power

A few additional cases, where the state has attempted to regulate the activities of federal contractors under the police power as such, also have some pertinence to our subject. Here, too, the basic doctrine is that of immunity for federal activities. This thinking is perhaps best displayed in the case of *Johnson v. Maryland*,[67] where the State of Maryland attempted to prosecute a Post Office Department employee for driving a postal truck within its jurisdiction without a state motor vehicle operator's license while delivering mail. The Court held this to be an invalid interference with a federal function. The case contains the aspects of an examination for competence, on the one hand, and the payment of a license fee, on the other, that are directly relatable to the independent contractor relationship as well. It will be noticed that, once more, the Court is willing to provide for non-conflicting exceptions. Yet it is fair to say that the area of allowable regulation by the state is not so clearly established by the decisions as is the scope of taxation for revenue in general:

In *Penn Dairies, Inc. v. Milk Control Commission*,[68] the Court sustained the refusal of the Pennsylvania Milk Control Commission to renew the license of a milk dealer who, in violation of the state law, had sold milk to the United States for troops at a camp located on land belonging to the state, at below the minimum price established by the Milk Commission. The majority was unable to find a constitutional or federal legislative basis for immunity from price-fixing by the state.

Similarly, in *James Stewart & Co. v. Sadrakula*,[69] state safety regulations applicable to building-construction contractors were upheld by the Court as applied to a contractor engaged in the construction of a building for the federal government, where no conflicting federal requirements could be found.

In *Leslie Miller, Inc., v. Arkansas*,[70] the Court held, however, that a state contractor's licensing statute could not be enforced against a private contractor who had been awarded a federal contract to construct jet fueling facilities at an Air Force base in Arkansas, but who was not licensed in the state. Under the Armed Services Procurement Act, the selection of the "lowest responsible bidder" by the Department of Defense prohibited the state from "frustrating" federal determinations of responsibility, in the Court's view.

The Fourteenth Amendment and the
Doctrine of Incorporation

Perhaps the most interesting potential area of constitutional limitation upon the state's use of the power of taxation for regulatory purposes is to be found in the Fourteenth Amendment, where both due process and equal protection of the laws are required.[71] Certain provisions of the Bill of Rights, although originally intended only as protection against federal authority, have been held by the Court to be incorporated within the meaning of the Fourteenth Amendment; for example,[72] the prohibition against self-incrimination under the Fifth Amendment[73] and the prohibition against cruel and unusual punishments under the Eighth Amendment.[74] The concluding clause of the Fifth Amendment also provides: ". . . nor shall private property be taken for public use without just compensation." While this prohibition has also been deemed to be incorporated within the Fourteenth Amendment,[75] the Court has recently had occasion to address directly the contention that a tax could constitute a "taking." In *City of Pittsburgh v. Alco Parking Corp.,*[76] a decision of the Pennsylvania Supreme Court holding a 20 percent gross-receipts tax on nonresidential parking "an uncompensated taking of property contrary to Fourteenth Amendment due process" was reversed by the U.S. Supreme Court on the grounds that *neither* due-process provision was intended as a limitation upon the taxing power; that is, neither state nor federal.[77]

Yet due process has in fact been invoked against the state taxing power with some success in certain cases. In *Speiser v. Randall,*[78] the denial of a tax exemption by the State of California for refusal to subscribe to a loyalty oath was held invalid by the Court as a denial of both procedural due process and freedom of speech under the First Amendment, which was considered as incorporated within the meaning of the Fourteenth Amendment. In *Hoeper v. Tax Comm. of Wisconsin,*[79] the Court overturned a Wisconsin tax which, due to its progressivity, effectively taxed the joint income of a husband and wife at a rate higher than that of individual taxpayers; the reasoning being that the due-process clause of the Fourteenth Amendment forbade the taxation of one person's income or property by reference to those of another person.

Due process has also been successfully invoked where succession taxes have operated retroactively upon interests that have vested.[80] However, it will be recalled, retroactivity in taxation is not considered banned as such.[81]

In *Union Transit Co. v. Kentucky,*[82] the Court held that an attempt by a state to tax property with a situs outside its boundaries amounted to a deprivation of property without due process. It should be noted that there is no similar limitation upon the federal taxing power.[83] But a state may tax residents on income from rents on land located outside the state.[84]

State property-tax-apportionment formulas applied to railroads on the basis of track mileage may also be subject to due-process attack if much higher-value property is found to be located in other states.[85]

The Court also found that a special assessment tax on a railroad for the construction of a highway violated due process when the asserted benefit to be derived was largely offset by a loss of local freight and passenger traffic as a consequence of the same improvement.[86] Similarly, where a dry island was included within a drainage district and no benefit was possible, the special assessment tax was held to be a deprivation of property without due process of law.[87]

So far as general taxes are concerned, if a taxpayer is given an opportunity to test the validity of a tax at any time before it is final, whether the proceedings for review take place before a board having quasi-judicial character or before a tribunal provided by the state for the purpose of determining such questions, procedural due process is not denied.[88] Where special assessments are concerned, however, there is a right of personal appearance in the determination of the assessments, or else due process is violated.[89] Furthermore, if the area of the assessment district was not determined by the legislative body, a landowner has the right to be heard respecting benefits to his property before it can be included in the improvement district and assessed.[90]

Generally, there is no necessity for a hearing if the mode of special assessment resolves itself into a mathematical formula.[91] But where there is an attempt to assess a particular property with a proportion of the cost of a sewer without the use of some formula, the taxpayer has a right to be heard under due process.[92]

Overassessment in general real-property taxation has not been held to be violative of due process.[93] Nor was it found to be a violation to assess at full value land subject to a mortgage without deduction of the debt.[94]

It has long been established that the exercise of the taxing power must be based on a public purpose.[95] The U.S. Supreme Court has tended to rely upon the judgment of the state courts[96] in the determination of what is to be considered a public purpose.[97]

When it is, in fact, applicable, all agencies of state and local government are held to be covered by the scope of the due-process clause of the Fourteenth Amendment.[98] Furthermore, the clause appears to offer potential protection against arbitrary action where no specific constitutional guarantee is found to exist.[99]

Equal Protection and Classification

The equal protection clause of the Fourteenth Amendment might be expected to have very special significance with regard to the exercise of the power of taxation by state and local government, particularly where schemes of classification are employed. It may come as somewhat of a surprise, therefore, to find Professor Corwin concluding: "The clause is least effective as a restraint on the taxing power of the States. Almost any classification made in a tax measure will be sustained by the Court, whether it is relevant to the business of raising revenue or proceeds from some ulterior motive."[100] In *Allied Stores of Ohio v. Bowers*,[101] the Court remarked: ". . . the States, in the exercise of their taxing power, are subject to the requirements of the equal protection clause of the Fourteenth Amendment. But that clause imposes no iron rule of equality, prohibiting the flexibility and variety that are appropriate to reasonable schemes of taxation. The State may impose different specific taxes . . . and may vary the rate of excise. . . . It is not required to resort to close distinctions or to maintain a precise, scientific uniformity with reference to composition, use or value. . . . But there is a point beyond which the State cannot go without violating the equal protection clause. The State must proceed upon a rational basis and may not resort to a classification that is palpably arbitrary."[102]

It is interesting to compare the Court's thinking here with its attitude on the question of regulation in general, as represented by its opinion in *Railway Express Agency, Inc. v. New York*,[103] where Justice Jackson wrote: "I regard it as a salutory doctrine that cities, States and the Federal Government must exercise their powers upon some reasonable differentiation fairly related to the object of regulation."

The State's latitude of discretion is wide where the classification of property for taxation purposes is concerned, as it is in the granting of total or partial exemptions on policy grounds.[104] However, intentional and systematic undervaluation by state officials of other taxable property in the same class violates the right of equal protection of those persons taxed upon the full value of their property.[105] This does not mean that mere errors in judgment that are neither intentional nor systematic resulting in unequal under- or overvaluation violate equal protection.[106] Owners discriminated against are entitled to have their assessment reduced to the common level.[107] Equal protection is violated if the state does not itself remove the discrimination; it cannot impose upon the person discriminated against the burden of seeking the upward revision of assessments of other members of the same class.[108]

In the case of special assessment taxation, equal protection is not violated where apportionment is made on an ad valorem basis; nor does general benefit to the community, as opposed to special benefit, imply a violation of the clause.[109] However, it has been held that railroad property may not be burdened for local improvements on a basis substantially different from that of individual owners, so as to produce manifest inequality.[110]

Similarly, a special highway assessment against railroads that included real property, rolling stock, and other personal property violated equal protection where other assessments for the same improvement were based upon real property alone.[111]

As can be seen, under the "traditional" view of equal protection there exists a clear presumption in favor of "reasonable" classifications; "invidious" discrimination would need to be found in order to offend the Constitution.[112] However, there is also to be considered here the so-called "new" equal protection, which came to arise from situations suggesting there might be certain classifications that, by their nature, were "suspect"[113] or affected "fundamental" rights or interests.[114] In such cases, "strict scrutiny" was indicated, and the usual presumption of validity was modified, requiring instead a showing of "compelling state interest" to uphold the measure in question. Thus arose the "two-tier" system of review, as it is now referred to, treating other sets of interests somewhat differently than those usually related to economic regulation.[115]

A most interesting application of the new rules arose with regard to taxation and issues involving equality in public education. Beginning with *Serrano v. Priest*,[116] the California Supreme Court held that a state school financing system that depended heavily upon local ad valorem taxation of property to supplement state aid was unconstitutional as a violation of federal equal-protection standards. Due to the widely varying tax base from one school district to another, the state court found that there was invidious discrimination against the poor as to the quality of the schools that their children attended.[117] In doing this, it held that wealth was to be considered a suspect classification and education a fundamental interest. A number of state courts immediately took up this cause, holding similar local financing arrangements in violation of Fourteenth Amendment (new) equal protection.[118] The immediate significance of those decisions may be appreciated by considering the fact that all states except Hawaii have relied very heavily on local property taxation to finance their schools.

Subsequently, in *San Antonio Ind. School Dist. v. Rodriguez*,[119] the U.S. Supreme Court reversed the decision in the Texas case. The Court's opinion, delivered by Mr. Justice Powell for a divided Court,[120] reflected the reluctance of the majority to assume once more the role of overseer of the "social and economic legislation" of the states.[121] It rejected the idea that there should be strict judicial scrutiny of state and local taxation and fiscal planning by the Court, asserting that "some inequality" is not sufficient grounds for holding such measures invalid.[122]

If nothing else, the case indicates the wide latitude that the Court is now willing to allow the state and local governments in fiscal planning and the use of the power of taxation.[123] However, from a civil rights viewpoint, the case may be seen as something of a misfortune.[124] Nevertheless, it is hard to escape the conclusion that the prospect of uprooting a widespread local system of financing education without the realistic possibility of alternative state support must have weighed heavily upon the Court in arriving at its decision.

Federal equal protection has yet another aspect of special significance, which will be discussed in the next chapter, in view of its particular relationship to state constitutional requirements—that of uniformity and equality where classification is concerned.

Notes

1. *Supra*, pp. 27 and 31; chapter 2, note 1; chapter 4, notes 24 and 44.

2. "This Constitution, and the Laws of the United States which shall be made in Pursuance thereof...shall be the supreme Law of the Land. . . ." *McCulloch* was not in fact the first ruling of the Court on this subject; see *U.S. v. Fisher*, 2 Cr. 358 (1805), dealing with the priority of debt claims.

3. In *Van Brocklin v. Tennessee*, 117 U.S. 151 (1886), the state was prohibited from selling land for taxes levied when the United States was in ownership but had ceased to have an interest in same at the time of the sale.

It should also be recognized that art. IV, §3, cl. 2, of the Constitution can here be of concomitant importance, providing that: "The Congress shall have Power to dispose of and make all needful Rules and Regulations respecting the Territory or other Property belonging to the United States. . . ."

In *Lee v. Osceola Imp. Dist.*, 268 U.S. 643 (1925), the Court held that a state could not assess land in the hands of private owners for benefits from road improvements completed while the United States was in ownership.

See also *Clallam County v. U.S.*, 263 U.S. 341 (1923), prohibiting taxation of a federally owned corporation organized under state law for war purposes and under liquidation.

4. This was later to be confirmed in *Thomson v. Union Pacific R.R. Co.*, 9 Wall. 579 (1870), and *Union Pacific R.R. Co. v. Peniston*, 18 Wall. 5 (1873), upholding a state tax on federally chartered railroads. The case of *California v. Central Pacific R.R. Co.*, 127 U.S. 1 (1888), holding a state tax levied on the franchise of an interstate railway corporation chartered by Congress invalid, was not only based on commerce clause considerations, but was specifically distinguished from the two foregoing cases in that they involved a tax levied upon the property of the companies and not upon their franchises or operations. Cf. *Chase Manhattan Bank v. Finance Admin. of N.Y.C.*, 59 L.Ed.2d 445 (1979), holding invalid New York City commercial rent and occupancy tax on national bank.

5. 4 Wheat. 316, 436. In terms of historical background, it was clear enough to the Court as well as all parties concerned that, by taxation, Maryland was erecting obstructionist regulatory measures against the National Bank, together with other states of similar antifederalist sympathies—the later *Veazi Bank* case, in reverse. *Supra* p. 27. For a concise review of these matters, see Cushman, *Constitutional Law* (5th ed., 1979) at 122-123.

It can thus be seen from what has been related that Justice Marshall was careful not to go further than needed in refutation of concurrent taxing powers.

6. 9 Wheat. 738 (1824).

7. See Corwin *supra* chapter 2, note 31, at 39-40, 277-279.

8. 306 U.S. at 487. Discussed *supra* page 8 and chapter 2, note 37.

9. 299 U.S. 401 (1937), where the salaries of the Panama Railroad Co. employees had been held exempt from New York State income tax as derived from a federal instrumentality.

10. 16 Pet. 435 (1842), where an income tax levied by Erie County on the salary of the captain of a federal revenue cutter was held invalid as a tax upon a government "means".

11. 302 U.S. 134 (1937). But see *Kern-Limerick v. Scurlock*, 347 U.S. 110 (1954), holding a gross-receipts tax invalid when applied to a contractor purchasing articles acting as agent for the federal govenment with title to pass directly from the vendor to the United States. The *Kern-Limerick* case, while not currently overruled, appears to have been substantially weakened by the following decisions: In *U.S. v. City of Detroit*, 355 U.S. 466 (1958), the Court upheld the following taxes imposed on federal contractors: (1) a municipal tax levied pursuant to a state law which stipulated that when tax-exempt real property is used by a private firm for profit, the firm is subject to taxation to the same extent as if it owned the property, and based upon the value of real property, a factory, owned by the United States and made available under a lease permitting the contracting corporation to deduct such taxes from rentals paid by it; the tax was collectible only by direct action against the contractor for a debt owed and was not applicable to federal properties on which payments in lieu of taxes are made; (2) a municipal tax, levied under the authority of the same state law, based on the value of the realty owned by the United States and collected from a cost-plus-fixed-fee contractor, who paid no rent but agreed not to include any part of the cost of the facilities furnished by the government in the price of goods supplied under the contract; (3) another municipal tax levied in the same state against a federal subcontractor and computed on the value of materials and work in process in his possession, notwithstanding that title thereto had passed to the United States following his receipt of installment payments; similarly, *City of Detroit v. Murray Corp.*, 355 U.S. 489 (1958), decided together with the foregoing "Borg Warner" case. The Court attempted to distinguish *U.S. v. Allegheny County*, 322 U.S. 174 (1944),

where the federal government had leased machinery to the contractor and it was taxed at full value under the Pennsylvania law, effectively taxing the federal government directly by an aggregate ad valorem tax on land and machinery.

12. 327 U.S. 474 (1946).

13. 314 U.S. 1 (1941).

14. 312 U.S. 176 (1941).

15. 308 U.S. 358 (1939).

16. *Susquehanna Power Co. v. Tax Comm.* (No. 1), 283 U.S. 291 (1931).

17. *Baltimore Shipbuilding Co. v. Baltimore*, 195 U.S. 375 (1904).

18. *Des Moines Bank v. Fairweather*, 263 U.S. 103, 106 (1923); *Owensboro National Bank v. Owensboro*, 173 U.S. 664, 669 (1899); *First National Bank v. Adams*, 258 U.S. 362 (1922); *Michigan National Bank v. Michigan*, 365 U.S. 467 (1961).

19. 297 U.S. 209 (1936).

20. 318 U.S. 357, 362 (1943).

21. 308 U.S. 21 (1939).

22. 314 U.S. 95 (1941).

23. *Federal Land Bank v. Kiowa County*, 368 U.S. 146 (1961).

24. 342 U.S. 232 (1952).

25. 336 U.S. 342 (1949), overruling a number of cases to the contrary.

26. The clause does not apply to lands acquired for forests, parks, ranges, wild life sanctuaries, or flood control, although a state may convey and Congress accept either exclusive or qualified jurisdiction over property within a state for other purposes. *Collins v. Yosemite Park Co.*, 304 U.S. 518, 528, 530 (1938).

In *Colorado v. Toll*, 268 U.S. 228 (1925), the Court held that a state may reserve the power of regulating roads in a national park where the land had been ceded to the federal government. In this case the park superintendent of Rocky Mountain National Park had attempted to exclude auto vehicles for hire from the park, and the state asserted its right to regulate bus service. The decision required a showing of state cession of such powers to the federal government, which was not met.

27. 376 U.S. 369 (1964). See also *Surplus Trading Co. v. Cook*, 281 U.S. 647 (1930).

28. Following a similar holding in *U.S. v. Allegheny County, supra* note 11.

29. *Mason Co. v. Tax Comm.*, 302 U.S. 186 (1937); See also, *Atkinson v. Tax Comm.*, 303 U.S. 20 (1938).

30. *Supra* note 11. See Corwin, *supra* Ch. 2, note 31 at 120 and cases cited therin.

31. *Id.*

32. 362 U.S. 628 (1960).

33. 327 U.S. 558 (1946).

34. *Northern Pacific R.R. Co. v. Myers*, 172 U.S. 589 (1899); *New Brunswick v. U.S.*, 276 U.S. 547 (1928).

35. *Irwin v. Wright*, 258 U.S. 219 (1922). Reference is to the reclamation of arid land by the federal government, where a lien exists on patents for charges payable. The Court held that the state may tax the equitable title although the legal title did not pass, but it may not tax until the equitable title passes. A special distinction would be found in the case of mining claims, since they are based on discovery and location; the right to remove would be taxable. Special conditions of reclamation and homesteading acts may be required to be met before the equitable interest is taxable by the state. For example, the homesteading act may require final certification of compliance with payments; similarly, equitable title to a farm unit will not be taxable until final size is known. (Entry and cultivation for five years required to perfect.) Regarding mining claims, cf. *Elder v. Wood*, 208 U.S. 226 (1908), where it was held that the right of possession alone is taxable and a patent unnecessary. See also *Forbes v. Gracy*, 94 U.S. 762 (1876), where the interest is regarded as personal property and not related to U.S. title.

36. 361 U.S. 376 (1960).

37. 365 U.S. 744 (1961).

38. See *South Carolina v. U.S.*, 199 U.S. 437 (1905), where the test was used to uphold federal taxing of state liquor dealers. As previously indicated, this application to the state taxing context was rejected in *Federal Land Bank of St. Paul v. Bismark Lumber Co., supra* page 41, and note 22.

39. This was similarly rejected in *Alabama v. King & Boozer, supra* page 41, and note 13, overruling *Panhandle Oil Co. v. Mississippi*, 277 U.S. 218 (1928), where the Coast Guard and a veteran's hospital had been held exempt from state gasoline taxes.

40. Following the general trend established in *Graves v. New York ex rel. O'Keefe, supra* note 8. This move had been presaged by the Court's decision in *Fox Film Corp. v. Doyal*, 286 U.S. 123 (1932), where patents and copyrights were removed from exempt status as federal instrumentalities and held subject to state taxation.

41. Following the decision in *James v. Dravo Construction Co., supra* note 11, the Court upheld a state income tax on a federal contractor in *Atkinson v. Tax Commissioner, supra* note 29.

42. See Corwin, *supra* chapter 2, note 31, at 278, and cases cited therein. As a technical matter, it should be kept in mind that two sources may serve to provide immunity or exemption from state taxation: federal supremacy and basic sovereignty.

43. See Corwin, *supra* chapter 2, note 31, at 278, and cases cited therein.

44. It has been observed by some legal commentators that there is also in practice a consensual division of tax "territories" (that is, subjects) in which one jurisdiction will by custom not compete with the other, resulting in de facto patterns of preemption. See Zimmerman, *Tax Planning for*

Land Use Control, 5 Urban Lawyer 639 (1973).

45. Perhaps the clearest example here of a primary area of infringement is the regulation of land-use activities that may affect interstate commerce.

46. On the side of concurrent jurisdiction are the terms *sharing field, divesting,* and *assimilation.* Where supremacy is concerned, *preemption, supersession, ousting, exclusive, repugnant, substantial frustration* (or *interference*), *occupation of field, dominant federal interest,* and *primary national concern* are examples, among others.

47. 319 U.S. 411 (1943) (re taxing and spending).

48. 368 U.S. 297 (1961) (re commerce).

49. 373 U.S. 132 (1963). Cf. *Jones v. Rath Packing Co.,* 430 U.S. 519 (1977), invalidating state weight standards for packaging.

50. 405 U.S. 707 (1972).

51. The principle is traceable to *General Motors v. Washington,* 377 U.S. 436, 440 (1964), where the Court stated: "A careful analysis of the cases in this field teaches that the validity of a tax rests upon whether the State is exacting a constitutionally fair demand for that aspect of interstate commerce to which it bears a special relation. For our purposes the decisive issue turns on the operating incidence of the tax. In other words, the question is whether the State has exerted its power in proper proportion to appellant's consequent enjoyment of opportunities and protection which the State has afforded" (state tax on privilege of doing business).

52. 411 U.S. 624 (1973).

53. 362 U.S. 440 (1960). A more cogent statement of the Court's position on the relationship of interstate commerce as such is later found in *Pike v. Bruce Church, Inc.,* 397 U.S. 137, 142 (1970): "Where the statute regulates evenhandedly to effectuate a legitimate local public interest, and its effects on interstate commerce are only incidental, it will be upheld unless the burden imposed on such commerce is clearly excessive in relation to the putative local benefits." (But here an Arizona packing and labeling statute was held invalid where it prohibited bulk shipment to California without source identification of cantaloupes grown in Arizona. Probably the excessive cost required for constructing an extra plant for labeling makes the case distinguishable from *Sligh v. Kirkwood,* 327 U.S. 52 (1915), where the Court upheld state standards for Florida oranges.)

54. 302 U.S. 1 (1937).

55. *Id.* at 10.

56. *Id.* at 15. Cf. *Ray v. Atlantic Richfield Co.,* 435 U.S. 151 (1978), invalidating state safety regulation of oil tankers. Here it is important to go back to Justice Marshall's original principles set down, on the one hand, in *Gibbons v. Ogden, supra* chapter 2, note 40, where a New York steamboat monopoly granted to Robert Fulton and Robert Livingston was repudiated by the Court in the face of a U.S. coasting license having been issued to Gibbon, and, on the other, in *Wilson v. Black Bird Creek Marsh Co.,* 2 Pet. 245 (1829), where state legislation authorizing construction of a dam in a

small tidal creek was upheld as a health- and property-preservation measure, although navigation was in fact obstructed thereby.

The Court, building upon these two cases, in *Cooley v. Board of Wardens of the Port of Philadelphia*, 12 How. 299 (1851), allowed state pilotage licensing on the basis of the absence of conflicting federal regulation or the need for uniform or national control of the subject matter.

Following the reasoning of the *Cooley* case, the Court has permitted the states to exercise control over tolls and rates of ferries, bridges, and tunnels, although they are technically within the purview of interstate commerce. See *Port Richmond & Bergen Point Ferry Co. v. Hudson County*, 234 U.S. 317 (1914). This case must be seen in the important larger context of governmental rate-making, as evidenced by *Wabash, St. L. & P. Ry. Co. v. Illinois*, 118 U.S. 557 (1886), requiring uniform national rate regulation of interstate railroads, and resulting in the establishment by Congress shortly thereafter of the Interstate Commerce Commission, to be followed by many other such agencies, and by the "Minnesota Rate Cases," *Simpson v. Shepard*, 230 U.S. 352 (1913), permitting state rate-setting in *intra*state commerce.

57. 116 U.S. 517 (1886).

58. 260 U.S. 245 (1922).

59. 262 U.S. 172 (1923).

60. 274 U.S. 284 (1927).

61. 257 U.S. 265 (1921).

62. 257 U.S. 277 (1921). If the levy is delayed so that it does not fall on the capture and production but enters an interstate pipeline, it may not be so taxed. *Michigan-Wisconsin Pipeline Co. v. Calvert*, 347 U.S. 157 (1954).

63. 252 U.S. 23 (1920). However, the business of piping gas from one state to another may not be regulated by a state. *Missouri ex rel. Barrett v. Kansas Gas Co.*, 265 U.S. 298 (1924).

64. The Natural Gas Act of 1938, 52 Stat. 821, was held to supersede state regulation in *Interstate Gas Co. v. F.P.C.*, 331 U.S. 682 (1947), where sales were made within a state by a natural-gas-producing company to pipeline companies that transported the purchased gas to markets in other states, and not to so supersede in *Panhandle Pipe Line Co. v. Public Service Comm.*, 332 U.S. 507 (1947), where gas was sold to industrial consumers within the state by an interstate pipeline company.

65. 125 U.S. 530 (1888).

66. Pullman car company: *Pullman's Palace Car Co. v. Pennsylvania*, 141 U.S. 18 (1891).

Railways: *Pittsburgh, C., C. & St. L. R.R. Co. v. Backus*, 154 U.S. 421 (1894) (valuation based on ratio of the length of line within state to total length); *Nashville, C. & St. Louis Ry. v. Browning*, 310 U.S. 362 (1940) (such part of the value of the entire system, less the value of its local property, such as terminals, shops, and nonoperating real estate, as is represented by the ratio which the railway's mileage within the state bears to the total mileage); *Adams Express Co. v. Ohio*, 165 U.S. 194 (1894), reh. 166 U.S. 185 (1897) (property worth less than $70,000 taxed at more than half a million dollars using ratio of Ohio mileage to total mileage in all states was upheld, as being "at its value as it is in its organic relations," that is, values derived from interstate commerce!).

Pipelines: *Memphis Gas Co. v. Stone*, 335 U.S. 80 (1948) ("Franchise" tax measured by the value of capital in the state, as applied to a pipeline company, a part of whose line passed through the state, although it did no business there).

Cf. *Complete Auto Transit Co. v. Brady*, 430 U.S. 274 (1977), upholding tax on "privilege of doing business," and overruling *Spector Motor Service v. O'Connor,* 340 U.S. 602 (1951).

67. 254 U.S. 51 (1920).

68. 318 U.S. 261 (1943). On the same day, the Court held that California could not penalize a milk dealer for selling milk to the War Department at less than the state minimum fixed price, where sales and deliveries were made to a federal enclave ceded by the state. *Pacific Coast Dairy v. Dept. of Agriculture*, 318 U.S. 285 (1943). Similarly, *Paul v. U.S.*, 371 U.S. 245 (1963), where existing armed forces procurement policy required purchase at lowest price by competitive bidding.

69. 309 U.S. 94 (1940).

70. 352 U.S. 187 (1956).

71. The Fourteenth Amendment, §1 (last sentence) provides: "No State shall make or enforce any law which shall abridge the privileges or immunities of citizens of the United States; nor shall any State deprive any person of life, liberty or property, without due process of law; nor deny to any person within its jurisdiction the equal protection of the laws."

The Fourteenth and Fifth Amendments both have a due-process clause. As previously indicated, the Fifth Amendment contains no equal protection provision. Certain differences may also exist between the due-process clauses themselves because of the tendency toward strict construction, insofar as the states are concerned, where the regulatory (police) power and taxing power are general, as opposed to the specifically enumerated and circumscribed powers of the federal government, where a more liberal attitude is considered more appropriate by the courts. See Corwin, *supra* chapter 2, note 31, at 388 and 462. The inheritance and estate tax cases of *Hoeper v. Tax Comm. of Wisconsin*, 284 U.S. 206 (1931) (invalidating) and *Fernandez v. Weiner, supra* chapter 2, note 9 (upholding), based on marital relationship, are thought to be distinguishable on these grounds. See Corwin, *id*. at 542.

To understand the background of the Court's present attitude, toward due process, eschewing for the most part interference with economic regulation by the states, the case of *Nebbia v. New York*, 291 U.S. 502 (1934), where the Court sustained a New York statute that regulated milk prices in the state, should be read.

Possible significance for the privileges and immunities portion of the Fourteenth Amendment is mentioned *infra*, pp. 91-92. As a potential constraint on discrimination against nonresidents, it must be read together with the seemingly similar provisions of art. IV, §2, cl. 1. See *Ward v. Maryland*, 12 Wall. 418 (1871). Cf. *Travis v. Yale & Towne Mfg. Co.*, 252 U.S. 60 (1920); *Travelers' Ins. Co. v. Connecticut*, 185 U.S. 364 (1902); *Madden v. Kentucky*, 309 U.S. 83 (1940), and particularly *Baldwin v. Montana Fish & Game Comm.*, 436 U.S. 371 (1978).

72. For present purposes, the question of "full" versus "selective" incorporation of the Bill of Rights within the Fourteenth Amendment need not be fully examined. With but one exception that is pertinent to our discussion (see note 74), most of the important aspects of the Bill of Rights have been incorporated judicially. For a complete tabulation of the status of the provisions, see *The Constitution of the U.S.A.*, Congressional Research Service, Library of Congress (1973), at 900-907. See also Corwin, *supra* chapter 2, note 25, at 251.

73. *Malloy v. Hogan*, 378 U.S. 1 (1964); *Murphy v. Waterfront Comm.*, 378 U.S. 52 (1964); *Griffin v. California*, 380 U.S. 609 (1965).

74. *Louisiana ex rel. Francis v. Resweber*, 329 U.S. 459 (1947); *Robinson v. California, supra* chapter 3, note 4. The full text of the amendment reads: "Excessive bail shall not be required, nor excessive fines imposed, nor cruel and unusual punishments inflicted." The pertinent exception referred to in note 72, *supra*, relates to excessive fines, which currently appears to be in a state of uncertainty with regard to Fourteenth Amendment incorporation. However, as will be seen in chapter 6, many state constitutions contain specific prohibitions against excessive fines.

75. *Chicago, B. & Q. R.R. v. City of Chicago*, 166 U.S. 266 (1897); *Fallbrook Irrigation District v. Bradley*, 164 U.S. 112 (1896); *Missouri Pacific Ry. v. Nebraska*, 164 U.S. 403 (1896).

76. 417 U.S. 369 (1974).

77. Corwin, *The Constitution, supra* chapter 2, note 31, at 42-43. For the previous discussion of this subject from the standpoint of the federal taxing power, see *supra* p. 8, and accompanying notes. The *McCray* case, *supra* pp. 27-28, also dealt with this contention in the negative.

78. 357 U.S. 513 (1958).

79. *Supra* note 71.

80. *Coolidge v. Long*, 282 U.S. 582 (1931).

81. *Welch v. Henry*, 305 U.S. 134 (1938). Reference is made to the discussion of the *Brushaber* case, *supra* chapter 2, note 29.

82. 199 U.S. 194 (1905); *Guarantee Trust Co. v. Virginia*, 305 U.S. 19 (1938).

83. *U.S. v. Bennett*, 232 U.S. 299 (1914); *Cook v. Tait*, 265 U.S. 47 (1924).

84. *New York ex rel. Cohn v. Graves*, 300 U.S. 308 (1937). In *Great Atlantic & Pacific Tea Co. v. Grosjean*, 301 U.S. 412 (1937), the Court upheld a license tax on chain stores at a rate per store determined by the number of stores both within and without the state, as not a tax in part upon things beyond the jurisdiction of the state.

85. *Wallace v. Hines*, 253 U.S. 66 (1920). See also the discussion with regard to commerce-clause considerations, *supra* page 47 and note 66.

86. *Road Imp. Dist. v. Missouri Pacific R.R. Co.*, 274 U.S. 188 (1927).

87. *Myles Salt Co. v. Iberia Drainage District*, 239 U.S. 478 (1916).

88. *Hodge v. Muscatine County*, 196 U.S. 276 (1905).

89. *Londoner v. Denver*, 210 U.S. 373 (1908). See also *St. Louis Land Co. v. Kansas City*, 241 U.S. 419 (1916); *Paulsen v. Portland*, 149 U.S. 30 (1893); *Bauman v. Ross*, 167 U.S. 548 (1897).

90. *Fallbrook Irrigation Dist. v. Bradley, supra* note 75, at 168, 175; *Browning v. Hooper*, 269 U.S. 396 (1926).

91. *Hancock v. Muskogee*, 250 U.S. 454 (1919).

92. *Paulsen v. Portland, supra* note 89.

93. *Nashville, C. & St. L. Ry. v. Browning, supra* note 66.

94. *Paddell v. New York*, 211 U.S. 446 (1908).

95. *Loan Association v. Topeka*, 20 Wall. 655 (1875); *Jones v. Portland*, 245 U.S. 217 (1917); *Green v. Frazier*, 253 U.S. 233 (1920); *Carmichael v. Southern Coal & Coke Co.*, 300 U.S. 644 (1937).

96. The attitude toward the federal exercise of the power is similar. See Corwin, *supra* chapter 2, note 31, at 401.

97. *Milheim v. Moffat Tunnel District*, 262 U.S. 710 (1923). Cases exhibit a variety of subjects within scope of public use: *Jones v. Portland* (coal and fuel yards); *Green v. Frazier* (warehouses, flourmills, elevators, homebuilding projects), both *supra* note 95; *Milheim v. Moffat Tunnel District* (railroad tunnels), *id.*

98. *Ex parte Virginia*, 100 U.S. 339 (1880); *Yick Wo v. Hopkins*, 118 U.S. 356 (1886); *Trenton v. New Jersey*, 262 U.S. 182 (1923); *U.S. v. Classic*, 313 U.S. 299 (1941); *Screws v. U.S.*, 325 U.S. 91 (1945).

99. Corwin, *supra* chapter 2, note 31, at 483, and cases cited therein.

100. Corwin, *supra* chapter 2, note 31, at 517. See *State Tax Com'rs. v. Jackson*, 283 U.S. 527 (1931); *Great Atlantic & Pacific Tea Co. v. Grosjean, supra* note 84.

101. 358 U.S. 522, 526-527 (1959). The power of the state to classify for purposes of taxation is ". . . of wide range and flexibility." *Louisville Gas Co. v. Coleman*, 277 U.S. 32 (1928). Certain industries and forms of industries may be favored by classification. *Quong Wing v. Kirkendall*, 223 U.S. 59 (1912); *Hammond Packing Co. v. Montana*, 233 U.S. 331 (1914); *Allied Stores of Ohio v. Bowers, id.* Different types of taxpayers may be taxed differently, despite the fact that they may compete. *Puget Sound Co.*

v. Seattle, 291 U.S. 619 (1934). But a gross sales tax graduated at rates increasing with the volume of sales has been held to violate equal protection. *Stewart Dry Goods v. Lewis*, 294 U.S. 550 (1935). Also, a heavier license tax on each unit in a chain of stores, only where the owner has stores located in more than one county, was held to violate the clause. *Liggett Co. v. Lee*, 288 U.S. 517 (1933). (This case was distinguished in *Great Atlantic & Pacific Tea Co. v. Grosjean, supra* note 84.)

    For an extensive review of cases dealing with classification and the equal-protection clause, see *The Constitution of the U.S.A., supra* note 72, at 1478-1480.

    102. See also *Flores v. Government of Guam*, 444 F2d 284, 288 (1971).

    103. 336 U.S. 106, 112 (1949). (New York City ordinance that regulated advertising on vehicles upheld).

    104. *F.S. Royster Guano Co. v. Virginia*, 253 U.S. 412 (1920). This is the case whether the exemption results from the terms of the statute or from the action of a state official under it. *Missouri v. Dockery*, 191 U.S. 165 (1903).

    105. *Sunday Lake Iron Co. v. Wakefield*, 247 U.S. 350 (1918); *Raymond v. Chicago Traction Co.*, 207 U.S. 20 (1907).

    106. *Coutler v. Louisville & Nashville R.R. Co.*, 196 U.S. 599 (1905). See also *Chicago, B. & Q. Ry. Co. v. Babcock*, 204 U.S. 585 (1907).

    107. *Sioux City Bridge v. Dakota County*, 260 U.S. 441 (1923).

    108. *Hillsborough v. Cromwell,* 326 U.S. 620 (1946).

    109. *Memphis & Charleston Ry. v. Pace*, 282 U.S. 241 (1931).

    110. *Kansas City So. Ry. v. Road Imp. Dist. No. 6*, 256 U.S. 658 (1921); *Thomas v. Kansas City So. Ry.*, 261 U.S. 481 (1923).

    111. *Road Imp. Dist. v. Missouri Pacific R.R. Co., supra* note 86.

    112. The traditional rules were carefully set down in *Lindsley v. Natural Carbonic Gas Co.*, 220 U.S. 61 (1911): "(1) The equal protection clause of the Fourteenth Amendment does not take from the State the power to classify in the adoption of police laws, but admits of the exercise of a wide scope of discretion in that regard, and avoids what is done only when it is without any reasonable basis and therefore is purely arbitrary. (2) A classification having some reasonable basis does not offend against that clause merely because it is not made with mathematical nicety or because in practice it results in some inequality. (3) When the classification in such a law is called in question, if any state of facts reasonably can be conceived that will sustain it, the existence of that state of facts at the time the law was enacted must be assumed. (4) One who assails the classification in such a law must carry the burden of showing that it does not rest upon any reasonable basis, but is essentially arbitrary." Cf. *Morey v. Doud,* 354 U.S. 457 (1957), overruled by *New Orleans v. Dukes*, 427 U.S. 297 (1976), upholding ordinance banning pushcarts in French Quarter.

    113. The principal foundation was laid in cases such as *Korematsu v.*

U.S., 323 U.S. 214 (1944), where the Court, although permitting the wartime evacuation of Japanese-Americans on the basis of national-security concerns, admitted that such measures were "immediately suspect" and subject to "rigid scrutiny," since they involved only a single ethnic-racial group.

114. This aspect of the new equal-protection formula probably arose from *Skinner v. Williamson*, 316 U.S. 535 (1942), where fundamental rights involving the compulsory sterilization of criminals were raised.

115. So far, "suspect" classifications seem to involve race and alienage or nationality; others of at least doubtful nature include sex, illegitimacy, wealth, or indigency. On the other hand, "fundamental" interests have included the rights to travel, to vote, to be free of wealth distinctions in the criminal process, and those interests relating to procreation. By no means does this list appear to be fixed. Protective, or "benign," discrimination that is corrective of past injustices may be freed of the constitutional ban. In *Kahn v. Shevin*, 416 U.S. 351 (1974), the Court upheld a Florida property tax exemption for widows, but not widowers, on the ground that it was ". . . reasonably designed to further the state policy of cushioning the financial impact of spousal loss upon the sex for whom that loss imposes a disproportionately heavy burden." The Court emphasized that women as a group, because of historic discrimination against them in the job market and elsewhere, provided a rational classification. See also *Schlesinger v. Ballard*, 419 U.S. 498 (1975), upholding promotional advantages for women Navy officers on similar grounds. The question may be raised whether the proposed Twenty-seventh or "Equal Rights Amendment" to the U.S. Constitution would place sex within the "fundamental" category.

Race appeared to be accorded somewhat different treatment in *Regents of the University of California v. Bakke*, 438 U.S. 265 (1978), the so-called "reverse discrimination" case involving the allocation of a fixed number of places in the University of California, Davis, Medical School under a special minority admissions program. The U.S. Supreme Court struck down the numerical features of the program, while at the same time approving the concept of "affirmative action". The significance of this complex decision with regard to the general questions of classification and equal protection under the Fourteenth Amendment is yet to be fully understood; six separate opinions produced separate majorities on two basic matters, with Justice Powell writing the opinion and acting as "swing vote" in each instance. See also *DeFunis v. Odegaard*, 416 U.S. 312 (1974), relating to law school, but mooted. Numerical "goals" or "quotas" outside the sphere of education (for example, construction workers) have not necessarily been disavowed by the *Bakke* case, however. See 92 Harv. L.Rev. 131 (Nov. 1978). Cf. *United Jewish Orgs. v. Carey*, 430 U.S. 144 (1977), upholding remedial discrimination in voting redistricting.

116. 5 Cal. 3d. 584 (1971).

117. The case is discussed in 49 J. Urb. L. 701 (1972); 1 Real Est. L.J. 115 (1972); 21 J. Pub. L. 23 (1972); 58 A.B.A.J. 120 (1972).

118. *Van Dusartz v. Hatfield*, 334 F.Supp. 870 (D.Minn. 1971); *Sweetwater Co. Plan. Comm. v. Hinkle*, 491 P.2d 1234 (Wyo. 1971): *Shofstall v. Hollins*, No. C-253652 (Ariz.Super.Ct. 1972), rev. 110 Ariz. 88 (1973); *Robinson v. Cahill*, 118 N.J. Super. 223 (1972) (invalidity ultimately based on New Jersey Constitution), 62 N.J. 473 (1973); *Milliken v. Green*, 389 Mich. 1 (1972), reh. 390 Mich. 389 (1973); *Rodriguez v. San Antonio School Dist.*, 337 F.Supp. 280 (W.D. Tex. 1971).

119. 411 U.S. 1 (1973), reh. den. 411 U.S. 959 (1973). The validity of *Serrano et al.* is called into question. The Court noted: "Rather than focusing on the unique features of the alleged discrimination, the courts in these cases have virtually assumed their findings of a suspect classification through a simplistic process of analysis: since, under the traditional systems of financing public schools, some poorer people receive less expensive educations than other more affluent people, these systems discriminate on the basis of wealth. This approach largely ignores the hard threshold questions . . ." (whether there is an identifiable class of disadvantaged poor and whether there is absolute rather than relative deprivation). "Before a State's laws and the justifications for the classifications they created are subjected to strict judicial scrutiny, we think these threshold considerations must be analyzed more closely. . . ." *Id.* at 19. See also *id.* at 23, 28 (Court note no. 65).

120. 5-4, with Justices Brennan, White, Douglas, and Marshall dissenting.

121. This is to be seen together with the latter-day attitude toward "substantive due process" under the Fourteenth Amendment, as represented by the *Nebbia* case, mentioned *supra* note 71.

122. The Court found that there was insufficient showing that *basic minimum education* (sufficient to satisfy the Fourteenth Amendment) was not provided. Also (although this was a class action by Mexican-American parents), there was insufficient showing that a suspect class was discriminated against. This was because no correlation could be established between the poor, and tax-poor districts.

A more careful reading of the opinion indicates that by no means have either of the questions been resolved, particularly the matter of wealth as a suspect classification.

In preference to the rigid choice between requiring minimum rationality or compelling state interest in the two-tier approach, Justice Marshall has cogently argued (see his dissent, 411 U.S. at 98) for a "sliding scale" review, where the strictness of the rule would move along a scale determined by the classification utilized or the interest in question.

In any test, it would seem that state economic regulation would still require only minimum rationality, while race would carry heavy presumptions of invalidity. But considering the mixed assortment of decisions by the Court, it is to Justice Marshall's credit that his formula appears to make many of them more consistent. See, for example, *James v. Strange*, 407 U.S. 128 (1972) (indigency); *Harper v. Virginia Bd. of Elections*, 383 U.S. 663 (1966) (voting and ability to pay taxes); *Levy v. Louisiana*, 391 U.S. 68 (1968) (illegitimacy); *Reed v. Reed*, 404 U.S. 71 (1971) (sex); *Weinberger v. Weisenfeld*, 420 U.S. 636 (1975) (male sex discrimination, as opposed to female in the preceding case); see also Gunter, *Foreword: In Search of Evolving Doctrine on a Changing Court: A Model for a Newer Equal Protection*, 86 Harv. L. Rev. 1 (1972).

A case of special interest in this area is *Salyer Land Co. v. Tulare Water Storage District*, 410 U.S. 719 (1973), where the Court held valid a special-purpose district arrangement that limited voting to landowners and also weighted their votes according to the assessed valuation of their land for property tax purposes. This is to be distinguished from the "one person, one vote" approach, represented by cases such as *Hadley v. Junior College District*, 397 U.S. 50 (1970), as being a part of equal protection. The narrowness of the tax source seems to have overcome such factors as the exclusion of nonlandowning residents and lessees, and the granting of voting rights to nonresident landowners and landowners whether they are natural persons or not. Curiously, the Court appears to have applied traditional standards of equal protection in its decision. 410 U.S. at 730, 732.

123. 411 U.S. at 24: ". . . the Equal Protection Clause does not require absolute equality or precisely equal advantages." See citations in Court note no. 57; Court note no. 66 contains a listing of cases with reasonable distinctions that have been upheld by the Court.

124. For an extensive discussion of the case and its implications in this regard, see *Symposium: Future Directions for School Finance Reform*, 38 L. & Contemp.Prob. No. 3 (Wint.-Sp. 1974). Articles on the particular states are as follows: Washington, *id.* at 366; Michigan, *id.* at 350; California, *id.* at 333; New Jersey, *id.* at 312; Texas (*Rodrigues*), *id.* at 299, 383, 566. See also 1973 Sup. Ct. Rev. 33; 47 S.Cal. L.Rev. 943 (May, 1974) (bilingual children issue); 59 Cornell L.Rev. 519 (March, 1974) (handicapped children issue).

6

State Constitutional Provisions Relating to the Taxing Powers of States and Their Instrumentalities

Introduction

As already indicated in the preface to this volume, the material developed in this chapter is an attempt to draw a profile of the various state constitutional constraints on the use of taxation as an instrument of land-planning policy. Analysis of the constitutions of the fifty states and the Commonwealth of Puerto Rico revealed that there are about nineteen important clusters of constraints that can be readily categorized; these have been reduced to tabular form by jurisdiction, with current constitutional citations. Due to its great significance as a constraint on taxation for purposes of land regulation, the so-called uniformity-and-equality clause has been discussed in some greater depth. The treatment described herein is indicative of the analysis necessary to integrate the interpretive case law with the literal constitutional constraint provisions of this nature.

For immediate use as a research tool, the tables may be conveniently used in conjunction with the state constitutions section of *Shepard's Citations* to derive the pertinent cases on a comparative-law basis, with regard to either (1) all the constraints applicable in a particular jurisdiction or (2) all the applicable jurisdictions for a particular category of constitutional constraint.

The tables are similarly useful in determining whether or not a jurisdiction has a particular constraint provision and, also, how many and which jurisdictions have a particular category of constraint in their current constitutions.

The tables have been uniformly brought up to date as of January 1, 1979; therefore, one must henceforth be sure to update from that time.

Interrelationship of Powers

It has been pointed out[1] that the state's power of taxation is considered to be derived not from its constitution but directly from its sovereignty as such.[2] Thus, state constitutional provisions that may relate to a state's inherent power of taxation are by their nature technically, or potentially, constraints on that power, although, of course, they may merely refer to it.

Because there are also limitations upon the state's power of taxation through the Federal Constitution, we may find that there are, in fact, two standards operating simultaneously, requiring determination of the applicable standard according to the various precepts of constitutional construction that we have been discussing.

The same observations might be made with regard to the state's exercise of the police power, to the extent that the taxing mechanism is employed for regulatory purposes.

Since the state may exercise its taxing powers directly, or through three basic forms of "municipal entity,"[3] state constitutions may contain as many as four different sets of restrictions upon the power of taxation. The state itself may be restricted in a number of ways that will be discussed later. Restrictions upon its instrumentalities, however, are generically more concerned with the question of *delegation*, a matter which also will be mentioned further herein.

Uniformity and Equality Requirements

By far the most important type of state constitutional provision affecting the use of taxation for policy-related purposes is the so-called uniformity clause, which is applicable both to the state and to any of its instrumentalities. This clause has a number of variations in phrasing, sometimes actually containing the word *uniformity* and sometimes not, with the word *equal* very often also being included. Its basic purpose is apparent. Taken literally, it means everything must be taxed in the same way. Were it not for the further addition of such words as *upon the same class* (of subjects, or property, or words interpreted to that effect), the existence of a clause of this nature would make it difficult, if not impossible, to adjust effectively the impact of taxation to achieve or avoid certain land-planning consequences. In the absence of fiscal inducements and discouragements, no policy could be implemented except, of course, the singular policy of uniformity and equality.

The first volume of this study[4] contains abstracts of the more important constitutional provisions dealing with taxation. Several interesting things will be noted in a careful examination and comparison of those clauses that are found to relate to uniformity. First of all, while there are, indeed, many variations in wording, there appear to be certain definite, definable species or "types". Also, oddly enough, several different types will be included within the same constitution.

In his definitive work on uniformity and equality in state constitutions,[5] Professor Newhouse was able to identify and define nine separate species of uniformity clause, assigning to each a "type" number from one to nine in descending order of strictness; "Type X", however, referred to constitutions with no uniformity provisions at all. The prototype wording of each of the clauses is set forth in table 1.

There were, in fact, two equally important aspects to the Newhouse study. In addition to the aspect of phraseology, that is to say, the literal wording comparisons that have just been referred to, there was also the need to examine the *effective* uniformity requirement resulting from the addition of judicial interpretation. For this purpose, it was found possible to use three rules for evaluating the *effective* uniformity limitation:

1. Universality versus no universality;[6]
2. Absolute uniformity in effective rates[7] versus rates uniform within classes;
3. Ad valorem method only versus no ad valorem requirement.

Working out the possible sets of yes/no alternatives for these three judicial evaluations, seven "permutations"[8] were arrived at, as shown in table 2.[9]

It has been mentioned that several different uniformity provisions may be found in the same constitution. This has been the result of periodic revision of the state constitutions over the years since their first adoption.[10]

The fact that in many cases several provisions dealing with uniformity have been incorporated and allowed to exist side by side led Professor Newhouse to choose to refer to "uniformity structures,"[11] in preference to the use of a term that would denote singularity. Thus, in any given state where there is more than one uniformity provision, it is necessary to determine

Table 1
Uniformity Provisions in State Constitutions: Prototype Clauses

Type I.: Property shall be taxed according to its value.

Type II.: Property shall be taxed in proportion to its value.

Type III.: The legislature may impose proportional and reasonable assessments, rates, and taxes upon all persons and estates within the state.

Type IV.: There shall be a uniform rule of taxation.

Type V.: Taxation shall be equal and uniform.

Type VI.: The legislature shall provide by law for a uniform and equal rate of assessment and taxation.

Type VII.: Taxes shall be uniform upon the same class of *subjects*.

Type VIII.: Taxes shall be uniform upon the same class of *property*.

Type IX.: There shall be a fair distribution of the expense of government.

("*Type X*" would include several states that have no uniformity clause at all.)

Source: Newhouse, *Uniformity and Equality in State Constitutions* (University of Michigan, Michigan Legal Studies, 1959) at 609-610. Reproduced with permission.

which of several possible *literal* choices is to be given effective meaning.[12] Over and above this, the ultimate effective meaning is given by judicial interpretation. It must be recognized that, from state to state, the courts can and do give different meanings to identical terms. Nevertheless, the starting point must be to identify which of several existing possibilities in a given state constitution is the "basic" clause, and how other provisions relate to it.

Table 3A indicates the original state assignments made by Professor Newhouse to the clause types enumerated in table 1.[13]

Since the time this part of the study was done, a number of states have made basic changes in their constitutions, including their "uniformity structures". Therefore, it is necessary to review these in terms of their present

Table 2
Newhouse Classification of Effective Uniformity Limitations

1. There is an effective limitation of:	
a. universality;	(0)
b. absolute uniformity in effective rates;	(0)
c. ad valorem method only.	(0)
2. There is an effective limitation of:	
a. NO UNIVERSALITY;	(= −2)
b. absolute uniformity in effective rates;	
c. ad valorem method only.	
3. There is an effective limitation of:	
a. NO UNIVERSALITY;	(= −2)
b. absolute uniformity in effective rates;	
c. NO AD VALOREM REQUIREMENT	(= −1)
4. There is an effective limitation of:	
a. universality;	
b. RATES UNIFORM WITHIN CLASSES;	(= −4)
c. ad valorem method only.	
5. There is an effective limitation of:	
a. universality;	
b. RATES UNIFORM WITHIN CLASSES;	(= −4)
c. NO AD VALOREM REQUIREMENT.	(= −1)
6. There is an effective limitation of:	
a. NO UNIVERSALITY;	(= −2)
b. RATES UNIFORM WITHIN CLASSES;	(= −4)
c. ad valorem method only.	
7. There is an effective limitation of:	
a. NO UNIVERSALITY;	(= −2)
b. RATES UNIFORM WITHIN CLASSES;	(= −4)
c. NO AD VALOREM REQUIREMENT.	(= −1)

Source: Newhouse, *Uniformity and Equality in State Constitutions*, (University of Michigan, Michigan Legal Studies, 1959) at 675. Reproduced with permission. Value assignments implicit in the ranking (shown in parentheses), have been added by the editor, as discussed in note 9, and are not part of the original table.

Table 3A
Classification of States by Type of Uniformity Clause

Alabama	Type II (clause added)
Arizona	Type VIII
Arkansas	Type I (clause added)
California	Type II
Colorado	(Changed)
Connecticut	None (Type X)
Delaware	Type VII
Florida	(Changed)
Georgia	Type VII
Idaho	Type VII
Illinois	(Changed)
Indiana	Type VI
Iowa	None (Type X)
Kansas	Type VI
Kentucky	Type VIII
Louisiana	(Changed)
Maine	Type I
Maryland	Type VIII
Massachusetts	Type III
Michigan	(Changed)
Minnesota	Type VII
Mississippi	Type V
Missouri	Type VII
Montana	(Changed)
Nebraska	Type II
Nevada	Type VI
New Hampshire	Type III
New Jersey	Type IV
New Mexico	Type VII
New York	None (Type X)
North Carolina	Type VIII
North Dakota	Type VIII
Ohio	Type IV
Oklahoma	Type VII
Oregon	Type VII
Pennsylvania	Type VII
Rhode Island	Type IX
South Carolina	(New clause)
South Dakota	Type VIII
Tennessee	(New clause)
Texas	Type V
Utah	Type VI
Vermont	Type IX
Virginia	Type VII
Washington	Type VIII
West Virginia	Type V
Wisconsin	Type IV
Wyoming	Type V

Source: Adapted from Newhouse, *Uniformity and Equality in State Constitutions* (University of Michigan, Michigan Legal Studies, 1959). Listing represents items still in effect as of January 1, 1979.

relationship to the classification system set forth. Table 3B identifies the types of clauses found in the revised state constitutions and also includes new entries for the newly admitted states of Alaska (1959) and Hawaii (1959) and the admission to commonwealth status of Puerto Rico (1952), none of which were included in the study.[14]

Table 3B
Classification of States by Type of Uniformity Clause (Addendum)

Alabama	Clause added 1972 (Type VIII)[a] to Existing Type II
Alaska	None (Type X)
Arkansas	Clause added 1976 to Existing Type I[b]
Colorado	New clause 1956 (Type VIII)[c]
Florida	New constitution 1968 (Type I)[d]
Hawaii	None (Type X)
Illinois	New constitution 1970 (Type I or VIII)[e]
Louisiana	New constitution 1975 (Type VIII)[f]
Michigan	New constitution 1964 (Type I)[g]
Montana	New constitution 1972 (Type I)[h]
(Puerto Rico)	New commonwealth constitution 1952 (Type IV)[i]
South Carolina	New clause 1976 (Type VIII)[j]
Tennessee	New clause 1973 (Type VIII)[k]

Source: This table was first published in the American Law Institute/American Bar Association 1979 *Course of Study Materials on Taxation as a Land Use Control,* © 1978 by Michael M. Bernard table copyright.

[a]Alabama Constitution, amend. 373 to art. XI, § 217, provides: "... all taxable property within this state, not exempt by law, shall be divided into the following classes for the purposes of ad valorem taxation...."

[b]Arkansas Constitution, amend. 57 of 1976 provides for the classification of intangible personal property, or for taxation of same, on a basis other than ad valorem.

[c]Colorado Constitution, art. X, § 3, provides: "All taxes shall be uniform upon each of the various classes of real and personal property located within the territorial limits of the authority levying the tax...."

[d]Florida Constitution, art. VII, § 2, provides: "All ad valorem taxation shall be at a uniform rate within each taxing unit; except the taxes on intangible personal property may be at different rates...."

[e]Illinois Constitution, art. IX, § 4(a), provides: "... taxes upon real property shall be levied uniformly by valuation ascertained as the General Assembly shall provide by law." (Type I) *Id.,* § 4 (b), provides: "... counties with a population of more than 200,000 may classify or continue to classify real property for purposes of taxation. Any such classification shall be reasonable and assessments shall be uniform within each class." (Type VIII exception).

[f]Louisiana Constitution, art. VII, pt. II, § 18, provides: "Property subject to ad valorem taxation shall be listed on the assessment rolls at its assessed valuation which ... shall be a percentage of its fair market value. The percentage of fair market value shall be uniform throughout the state upon the same class of property."

[g]Michigan Constitution, art. IX, § 3, provides: "The legislature shall provide for the uniform general ad valorem taxation of real and personal property not exempt by law....

Table 3B *(continued)*

The legislature may provide for alternative means of taxation of designated real and tangible personal property *in lieu* of general ad valorem taxation. Every tax other than the general ad valorem property tax shall be uniform upon the class or classes on which it operates."

hMontana Constitution, art. VIII, § 4, provides: *"Equal valuation.* All taxing jurisdictions shall use the assessed valuation of property established by the state."

iPuerto Rico Constitution, art. VI, § 3, provides: "The rule of taxation in Puerto Rico shall be uniform." (Puerto Rico is not a state but has commonwealth status under compact.)

jSouth Carolina Constitution, art. X, § 1, provides: "The General Assembly may provide for the ad valorem taxation by the State or any of its subdivisions of all real and personal property. The assessment of all property shall be equal and uniform in the following classification. . . ."

kTennessee Constitution, art. 2, § 28, provides: " . . . all property real, personal or mixed shall be subject to taxation. . . .For purposes of taxation, property shall be classified. . . .The ratio of assessment to value of property in each class or subclass shall be equal and uniform throughout the State, the value and definition of property in each class or subclass to be ascertained in such manner as the Legislature shall direct. . . ."

In the second step of the Newhouse analysis, each state was classified according to the judicial position that had been taken on each of the three questions set forth in table 2 herein. The classification by states of effective limitation according to the seven possibilities enumerated is shown in table 4. Where the constitution has been substantially changed since the date of the study, a notation has been made to that effect.

In the final step of the Newhouse analysis, the *class* of *effective* uniformity limitation resulting from judicial interpretations was matched against the *literal* phraseology of the various clauses by *type.* This was displayed in a matrix format,[15] which is shown in somewhat edited form in table 5.[16] It was thus possible to view the distribution of the attributes according to four sectors: (A) strict literal/strict effective; (B) strict literal/liberal effective; (C) liberal literal/liberal effective; (D) liberal literal/strict effective. The conclusions that could be reached as a result of this analysis were that, while there was extensive variation within the sectors, with a minimal number of exceptions there was a direct correlation between the literal words and the effective limitation. It should be kept in mind that the dividing lines between sectors are Types I through VI for strict literal and Types VII through X for liberal literal, and Classes 1 through 3 for strict effective and Classes 4 through 7 for liberal effective.

It was found that the greatest diversity within sectors was in those states that had basic uniformity clauses which on their face were more susceptible of being construed to permit classification.[17] The greatest diversity was found to exist in the Type VII clause: "Taxes shall be uniform upon the same class of subjects."[18] In almost all cases where there was diversity in result among states having potentially liberal uniformity clauses (that is, permitting classification), the diversity was found to be related to the

Table 4

Classification of States by Effective Judicial Uniformity Limitation

Alabama	Class 2 (clause added)
Arizona	Class 5
Arkansas	Class 1 (clause added)
California[a]	Class 1
Colorado	(Changed)
Connecticut	None
Delaware	Class 7
Florida	(Changed)
Georgia	Class 5
Idaho	Class 2
Illinois	(Changed)
Indiana	Class 1
Iowa	None
Kansas[a]	Class 2
Kentucky	Class 4
Louisiana	(Changed)
Maine[a]	Class 2
Maryland	Class 4
Massachusetts	Class 2
Michigan	(Changed)
Minnesota	Class 7
Mississippi	Class 2
Missouri	Class 4
Montana	(Changed)
Nebraska[a]	Class 1
Nevada[a]	Class 1
New Hampshire	Class 2
New Jersey	Class 6
New Mexico	Class 4
New York	None
North Carolina	Class 4
North Dakota	Class 7
Ohio[a]	Class 1
Oklahoma	Class 7
Oregon	Class 7
Pennsylvania	Class 6
Rhode Island	Class 7
South Carolina	(New clause)
South Dakota	Class 7
Tennessee	(New clause)
Texas	Class 1
Utah	Class 1
Vermont	Class 7
Virginia	Class 5
Washington	Class 7
West Virginia[a]	Class 1
Wisconsin	Class 2
Wyoming	Class 2

Source: Adapted from Newhouse, *Uniformity and Equality in State Constitutions* (University of Michigan, Michigan Legal Studies, 1959) at 676-679.

Note: Classes 1, 2, and 3 are the strictest limitations. Effective limitations permitting classified property taxes would be Classes 4, 5, 6, and 7. However, only Classes 6 and 7 would permit the most flexible types of classified property tax, one under which free exemption is permitted.

Table 4 *(continued)*

Note: Alaska and Hawaii, both absent from the original compendium, were later to adopt constitutions with no uniformity clause.

aSome states have modified the effective limitation by amendment without altering the basic uniformity clause in its phraseology. These are so noted by Professor Newhouse. Other notations are the editor's.

addition of supplementary clauses to the constitution involved.[19] This was true even in cases where the basic clauses were found to be identical.[20] However, where potentially restrictive basic clauses were concerned, supplementary clauses were found not to create conflicts, but simply to serve to buttress the effective limitation of the basic clause itself.[21]

The foregoing tables are, of course, a necessary but great over-simplification[22] of state constitutional standards. To derive the maximum benefit for our purposes from the massive analytical effort represented by the Newhouse study, we should recognize some of the important underlying aspects that it was necessary to take into consideration regarding the application of uniformity requirements. The more important of these might be summarized as follows:

1. The application of uniformity requirements to *property* or *nonproperty* interests.
2. The question of what is defined or interpreted to fall within the meaning of the term *property* for taxation purposes.[23]
3. Whether *tangible* or *intangible* property[24] is subject to a uniformity requirement.
4. Whether *real* or *personal* property[24] is subject to a uniformity requirement.
5. The application of the uniformity requirement to (a) the object of taxation;[25] (b) the effective rate;[26] (c) the method of taxation.[27]
6. Whether classification provisions are applicable to (a) property;[28] (b) rates of taxation;[29] (c) exemptions.

It becomes clear enough from the foregoing that a state court is possessed of a great many options for arriving at its own interpretation of uniformity policy in taxation.

Relationship of the Federal Equal-Protection Clause to State Uniformity and Equality Requirements

It may be seen that state uniformity requirements can be derived from a state's equal-protection clause.[30] Thus it is that, in addition to the various aspects of federal equal protection that have already been discussed, a specific element of uniformity may be derived from the Fourteenth Amend-

Table 5

Comparative Analysis of Literal and Effective Property-Tax Uniformity Limitations

TYPES	*Effective Limitations (Classes):* (1) (a) YES (b) YES (c) YES	(2) (a) NO (b) YES (c) YES	(3) (a) NO (b) YES (c) NO	(4) (a) YES (b) NO (c) YES	(5) (a) YES (b) NO (c) NO	(6) (a) NO (b) NO (c) YES	(7) (a) NO (b) NO (c) NO
	Sector "A"			*Sector "B"*			
I. ARK	ARK						
ME		ME					
TENN	TENN						
II. CAL	CAL						
NEB	NEB						
III. MASS		MASS					
NH		NH					
IV. NJ							NJ
OHIO	OHIO						
WISC		WISC					
V. MISS		MISS					
TEX	TEX						
WVA	WVA[a]						
WYO		WYO					
VI. IND	IND[b]						
KAN		KAN					
NEV	NEV						
UTAH	UTAH						
	Sector "D"			*Sector "C"*			
VII. DEL							DEL
GA					GA[c]		
IDA		IDA					
MINN							MINN
MO				MO[c]			
NM				NM[d]			
OKLA							OKLA
ORE							ORE
PA						PA	
VA					VA		
VIII. ARIZ					ARIZ		
KY				KY			
MD				MD			
NC				NC			
ND							ND
SD							SD
WASH							WASH
IX. RI							RI
VT							VT
X. CONN							CONN
IOWA							IOWA
NY							NY

Source: Adapted from Newhouse, *Uniformity and Equality in State Constitutions* (University of Michigan, Michigan Legal Studies, 1959) at 677-678, with permission.

Note: Reading down, states are grouped according to types of uniformity clauses, the literal

Table 5 *(continued)*

limitations. Reading from left to right, classification is from strict to liberal effective uniformity limitation, depending on answers to three questions: (a) Is there a rule of universality? (b) Is absolute uniformity required of effective rates? (c) Is the ad valorem method required? Heavy lines separate strict from liberal limitations. The four sectors, reading clockwise, are: (A) strict literal/strict effective; (B) strict literal/liberal effective; (C) liberal literal/liberal effective; (D) liberal literal/strict effective.

aBy amendment, all property has been classified.

bA distinction is made between the terms *selection* and *exemption* of property. Where *selection* is used, the rule of universality is not held to apply.

cThe classification of rates is spelled out by an amendment. Doubt was also expressed as to the applicability of the ad valorem rule in Georgia.

dStrict rules apply only to the taxation of tangible property because of peculiar phraseology.

ment to the U.S. Constitution acting in concert with the various state requirements that we have just reviewed.[31] In fact, if we were to apply the Newhouse classification scheme to the federal equal-protection provision, the *effective* limitation created would be as follows: (a) no universality; (b) rates uniform within classes; (c) no ad valorem requirement. In other words, the federal provision would have the equivalent of a "Class 7" limitation within the context of the state analysis. This is borne out in a review of some of the more important cases that have been decided by the U.S. Supreme Court on the subject.[32]

It was found that in almost all state constitutions there existed some equivalent to an equal-protection limitation, even though less than half (currently, twenty-four) of the jurisdictions have literal clauses of this nature.[33] Taken together with this, the federal minimum standard forms the base requirement, regardless of the existence of any state constitutional uniformity provision as such.[34]

Thus, it may be said that there exists a minimum standard of uniformity to which state tax legislation must conform, apart from any state constitutional limitation, and that both the state and federal courts will together apply a minimum standard of reasonableness based on their own particular interpretation of equal protection.[35]

Due Process and Equal Protection

In the last section, equal protection was explored in a rather specialized context, relating it to state uniformity requirements. We must now consider the general protection afforded to all persons by due process and equal protection at the state as well as federal constitutional level against laws or actions by the state or its instrumentalities. In addition to the provisions found in the Fourteenth Amendment to the U.S. Constitution, each state may, in fact, provide for its own due-process clause or equal-protection clause, or both. In such circumstances, the courts of each of the states may interpret each of the clauses according to their own conceptions of the rights involved or the measures in question, independent of the federal judicial interpretation of the Fourteenth Amendment; that is, a state can impose a different, somewhat stricter rule if it is inclined to do so. These provisions therefore operate separately as additional potential constraints where the taxing powers of the states are concerned. State constitutional due process, then, may come into play, as may equal protection, in questions involving a regulatory or police-power use of taxation.

Thirty-eight jurisdictions have due-process clauses in their constitutions. Of the twenty-four jurisdictions mentioned that have equal-protection clauses, nineteen also have a due-process clause, of which eight are combined in the single clause form. Table 6 sets forth the principal provisions to be found in the state constitutions and the constitution of the Commonwealth of Puerto Rico.

Special Privileges or Immunities

There appears to be some overlapping in the protections afforded by due-process and equal-protection clauses and those furnished by clauses prohibiting special privileges or immunities. Prohibitions against special privileges or immunities are found in the constitutions of thirty-nine jurisdictions. Of these, ten relate to prohibitions against irrevocability only, although nonirrevocability provisions are found in a total of nineteen jurisdictions altogether. Table 7 lists the jurisdictions and citations to these constitutional provisions.

The Massachusetts constitution contains a type of provision[36] prohibiting "exclusive privileges," which may have a somewhat different scope than the standard phraseology noted in the table.

Excessive Fines

An interesting constitutional constraint of potential application is that relating to the prohibition against excessive fines. The classic expression is found, of course, in the Eighth Amendment to the U.S. Constitution, which reads as follows: "Excessive bail shall not be required, nor excessive fines imposed, nor cruel and unusual punishments inflicted." It is repeated with moderate variation in most of the state constitutions, with the specific prohibition that is most pertinent relating to fines appearing in forty-eight of the jurisdictions.

It is important to say *potential* application here, since the range of possible regulatory actions that may be undertaken through taxation is extremely broad.

Table 8 lists the jurisdictions and citations to the applicable constitutional provisions.

Separation of Powers

Where the exercise of the police power and the power of taxation tend to blend, state constitutional provisions dealing with the separation of powers would necessarily begin to take on more significance. Very many regulatory efforts, certainly in the modern context, have tended to enlist the executive establishment in the promulgation and administration of standards, among other things. As has already been pointed out,[37] the federal separation-of-powers doctrine does not impose a separation-of-powers requirement on state government.

Although forty states have more or less expressly provided for separation of powers in their constitutions, there is perhaps little question that the doctrine exists in one form or another in just about all of the jurisdictions. Table 9 lists the jurisdictions and citations to the applicable constitutional provisions.

Intergovernmental Distribution of Power

Separation-of-powers requirements are essentially concerned with *intra*-governmental distribution of power; that is, between the three classic *branches* of government. Perhaps the broadest set of constraints, however, arises from state constitutional provisions that, for our purposes, effectively distribute both the taxing and the police powers between the state and its various municipal entities. The constraints work up and down; in other words, both the state and its subordinate units are restricted in their powers. State powers may often be proscribed in a manner reminiscent of the federal constitutional format. A prime example of this is a common provision prohibiting the state (legislature) from enacting certain local or special laws. Table 10 lists clauses of this nature that contain provisions relating to the power of taxation.[38] However, delegation by the state to municipal bodies may be enjoined or partly limited, or municipalities may be given exclusive power. Most notably, the state may be excluded from the ad valorem taxation of real property. Table 11 lists such jurisdictions and the citations to the applicable constitutional provisions.

Table 6
Due-Process and Equal-Protection Clauses in State Constitutions

	Due Process[d]	Equal Protection
Alabama	Art. I, § 6	
Alaska	Art. I, § 7	Art. I, § 1
Arizona	Art. II, § 4	Art. II, § 13
Arkansas	Art. II, § 8	
California	Art. I, § 7	Id.
Colorado	Art. II, § 25	
Connecticut	Art. I, § 8	Art. I, § 20
Florida	Art. I, § 9	
Georgia	Art. I, § I, para. I	Art. III, § VIII, para. III[a]
Hawaii	Art. I, § 5	Id.
Idaho	Art. I, § 13	
Illinois	Art. I, § 2	Id.
Indiana		Art. I, § 23[b]
Iowa	Art. I, § 9	Art. I, § 6[b]
Kansas	B.Rts. § 18[c]	B.Rts. § 2[b]
Kentucky		B.Rts. § 3[b]
Louisiana	Art. I, § 2	Art. I, § 3
Maine	Art. I, § 6A	Id.
Maryland	D.Rts. art. 23[d]	
Michigan	D.Rts. Art. I, § 17	Art. I, § 2
Minnesota	Art. I, § 7	
Mississippi	Art. III, § 14	
Missouri	Art. I, § 10	
Montana	Art. II, § 17	
Nebraska	Art. I, § 3	
Nevada	Art. 1, § 8	
New Hampshire		Pt. I, art. 2[b]
New Mexico	Art. II, § 18	Id.
New York	Art. I, § 6	Art. I, § 11
North Carolina	Art. I, § 19[d]	Id.
North Dakota	Art. I, § 13	
Oklahoma	Art. II, § 7	
Ohio		Art. II, § 26[b]
Oregon		Art. I, § 20[b]
(Puerto Rico)	Art. II, § 7	Id.
South Carolina	Art. I, § 3	Id.
South Dakota	Art. VI, § 2	Art. VI, § 18
Texas	Art. I, § 19[c]	Art. I, § 3[b]
Utah	Art. I, § 7	
Virginia	Art. I, § 11	
Washington	Art. I, § 3	
West Virginia	Art. III, § 10	
Wyoming	Art. I, § 6	

[a]The Georgia Constitution contains a provision dealing with equal protection which may have special significance for regulatory measures: "The exercise of the police power of the state shall never be abridged, nor so construed as to permit the conduct of business in such manner as to infringe the equal rights of others, or the general well-being of the state." See also art. I, § II, para. III.

[b]There is some overlapping with clauses prohibiting special privileges and immunities; e.g., Indiana provides: "The General Assembly shall not grant to any citizen, or class of citizens,

Table 6 *(continued)*

privileges or immunities, which, upon the same terms shall not equally belong to all citizens." Other types of provisions overlap with general uniformity or general equality; e.g., Iowa: "All laws of a general nature shall have uniform operation"; New Hampshire: "Equality of rights under the law shall not be abridged by the state on account of race, creed, color, sex or national origin"; some may be combinations of any of these. See also Kansas, Kentucky, Ohio, Oregon, Texas, and Utah. Refer to table 7 for prohibitions against special privileges and immunities.

cThe wording *due course* is used instead.

dThe wording *law of the land* may be equivalent. Cf.: Del. art. I, § 7; Mass. D.Rts. art. XII; N.H. B.Rts. art. 15; Pa. art I, § 9; R.I. art I, § 10; Tenn. art. I, § 8; Vt. art. I, § 10. In Nov. 1978, Maryland renumbered art. 23 to art. 24.

Of course, the kind of "upward restriction" that is being discussed is, in a real sense, institutionalized by the concept of home rule. There are, in fact, forty states that have now enacted some constitutional provisions dealing with municipal charter government and home rule. A great deal of variety exists among the states in the structuring of local autonomy, with many complex considerations from the point of view of exercising *regulatory* taxing powers. It is fairly clear that each state's provisions must be individually addressed with regard to the extent of the resultant state or local power respecting a given subject matter. Table 12 sets forth the citations to the applicable provisions of the various jurisdictions setting up charter or home rule relationships in their constitutions.

In addition to the distribution-of-power considerations already mentioned, there also exist provisions defining and limiting the territorial jurisdiction of the various taxing agencies. Table 13 sets forth the states having constitutional provisions of this nature, and citations to those provisions. It should be noted that, in a number of instances, this requirement is found in the uniformity/equality clause of the constitution and relates thereto.

Prohibitions against Delegation, Surrender, Suspension, or Contracting Away of the Taxing Power

There exists an important family of state constitutional restrictions that includes prohibitions against delegation, surrender, suspension, or contracting away of the power of taxation. One group is concerned with preventing delegation to nongovernmental recipients. A second group relates to surrender, suspension, or contracting away of the taxing power to private corporations. A third group prohibits the surrender, suspension, or contracting away of the taxing power in general. These can become particularly important where commercial or developmental incentives are contemplated. A total of twenty-nine jurisdictions contain clauses of this nature. It is sometimes difficult to conceive that a sovereign power such as taxation may be contracted away in some circumstances, but there is no question that the precedent is there. As a matter of fact, this brings into play another prevalent constitutional provision that prohibits the impairing of the obligation of contracts (using language similar to U.S. Constitution, art. I, §10), which may prevent a state from changing its position if this action is or was once not prohibited and was taken. Twenty-five jurisdictions have provi-

Table 7

Prohibitions against Special Privileges or Immunities in State Constitutions

Alabama	Art. IV, § 104; art. I, § 22[a]
Alaska	Art. I, § 15[a]
Arizona	Art. II, §§ 9[a] and 13; art. IV, § 19 (13)
Arkansas	Art. II, § 18; art. II, § 3
California	Art. I, § 7 (b)
Colorado	Art. V, § 25; art. II, § 11[a]
Connecticut	Art. I, § 1
Florida	Art. III, § 11 (12)
Georgia	Art. I, § I, para. VII[a]
Hawaii	Art. I, § 21[a]
Idaho	Art. I, § 2[a]
Indiana	Art. I, § 23
Iowa	Art. VIII, § 12; art. I, § 6
Kansas	B.Rts. § 2[a]
Kentucky	B.Rts. § 3
Louisiana	Art. III, § 12 (7); art. XII, § 12
Minnesota	Art. XII, § 1
Missouri	Art. III, § 40 (28); art. I, § 13[a]
Montana	Art. II, § 31[a]
Nebraska	Art. III, § 18; art. I, § 16[a]
New Hampshire	Pt. I, art. 10
New Jersey	Art. IV, § VII, 9 (8)
New Mexico	Art. IV, §§ 24 and 26
New York	Art. III, §§ 17 and 21
North Carolina	Art. I, § 32
North Dakota	Art. I, § 20[a]; art. II, § 69 (20)
Ohio	Art. I, § 2[a]
Oklahoma	Art. V, § 51
Oregon	Art. I, § 20
Pennsylvania	Art. I, § 17[a]
(Puerto Rico)	Art. VI, § 13[a]
South Dakota	Art. VI, §§ 12[a] and 18; art. III, § 23 (9)
Tennessee	Art. XI, § 8
Texas	Art. I, § 3; art. I, § 17[a]
Utah	Art. I, § 23[a]
Vermont	Ch. I, art. 7
Virginia	Art. I, § 4; art. IV, § 14 (18)
Washington	Art. I, §§ 8[a] and 12
Wyoming	Art. I, § 3; art. III, § 27

[a]Prohibition relates to aspects of irrevocability.

sions prohibiting the contracting away of taxing powers, and forty-one prohibit impairing the obligation of contracts. However, a match-up of the
states would show that in only sixteen of them would the impairment provi-

Table 8
Prohibitions against Excessive Fines in State Constitutions

Alabama	Art. I, § 15
Alaska	Art. I, § 12
Arizona	Art. II, § 15
Arkansas	Art. II, § 9
California	Art. I, § 17
Colorado	Art. II, § 20
Connecticut	Art. I, § 8
Delaware	Art. I, § 11
Florida	Art. I, § 17
Georgia	Art. I, § I, para. XIV
Hawaii	Art. I, § 12
Idaho	Art. I, § 6
Indiana	Art. I, § 16
Iowa	Art. I, § 17
Kansas	B.Rts. § 9
Kentucky	B.Rts. § 17
Maine	Art. I, § 9
Maryland	D.Rts. art. 25
Massachusetts	D.Rts. Pt. I, art. 26
Michigan	D.Rts. art. I, § 16
Minnesota	Art. I, § 5
Mississippi	Art. III, § 28
Missouri	Art. I, § 21
Montana	Art. I, § 22
Nebraska	Art. I, § 9
Nevada	Art. 1, § 6
New Hampshire	Pt. I, art. 33
New Jersey	Art. I, § 12
New Mexico	Art. II, § 13
New York	Art. I, § 5
North Carolina	Art. I, § 27
North Dakota	Art. I, § 6
Ohio	Art. I, § 9
Oklahoma	Art. II, § 9
Oregon	Art. I, § 16
Pennsylvania	Art. I, § 13
(Puerto Rico)	Art. II, § 11
Rhode Island	Art. I, § 8
South Carolina	Art. I, § 15
South Dakota	Art. VI, § 23
Tennessee	Art. I, § 16
Texas	Art. I, § 13
Utah	Art. I, § 9
Virginia	Art. I, § 9
Washington	Art. I, § 14
West Virginia	Art. III, § 5
Wisconsin	Art. I, § 6
Wyoming	Art. I, § 14

sions have effective application.[39] Table 14 lists the jurisdictions with clauses prohibiting delegation, surrender, suspension, or contracting away of the taxing power, with notation as to which group is involved in each case. Where no footnote is indicated, all the prohibitions are represented therein. Table 15 lists the jurisdictions having constitutional provisions with prohibitions against impairment of obligation of contracts, and also indicates whether the constitution has a clause prohibiting the contracting

Table 9

Separation of Powers Requirements in State Constitutions

Alabama	Art. III, § § 42 and 43
Arizona	Art. III
Arkansas	Art. IV, § § 1 and 2
California	Art. III, § 3
Colorado	Art. III
Connecticut	Art. II
Florida	Art. II, § 3
Georgia	Art. I, § II, para. IV
Idaho	Art. II, § 1
Illinois	Art. II, § 1
Indiana	Art. III, § 1
Iowa	Art. III, § 1
Kentucky	§ § 27 and 28
Louisiana	Art. II, § § 1 and 2
Maine	Art. III, § § 1 and 2
Maryland	D.Rts. art. 8
Massachusetts	D.Rts. Pt. I, art. 30
Michigan	Art. III, § 2
Minnesota	Art. III, § 1
Mississippi	Art. I, § § 1 and 2
Missouri	Art. II, § 1
Montana	Art. III, § 1
Nebraska	Art. II, § 1
Nevada	Art. 3, § 1
New Hampshire	Pt. I, § 37
New Jersey	Art. III
New Mexico	Art. III, § 1
North Carolina	Art. I, § 6
Oklahoma	Art. IV, § 1
Oregon	Art. III, § 1
Rhode Island	Art. III
South Carolina	Art. I, § 8
South Dakota	Art. II
Tennessee	Art. II, § § 1 and 2
Texas	Art. II, § 1
Utah	Art. V, § 1
Vermont	Ch. II, § 5
Virginia	Art. I, § 5; art. III, § 1
West Virginia	Art. V, § 1
Wyoming	Art. II, § 1

away of the taxing power, either generally or to corporations, so that the effective application of the impairment clause may be seen.

"Arithmetic" Limitations on Taxation

The limitation that has recently received the most attention and has resulted in some of the most dramatic political changes is a variety that I have chosen to term "arithmetic" (currently, it is very often commonly referred to as a "cap"). California's so-called "Proposition 13" is, of course, the now-famous prototype. However, it is interesting to find that this is hardly a new sort of measure, and it may surprise many that no fewer than twenty-eight states already possessed some kind of arithmetic limitation when

Table 10
Prohibitions against Special or Local Laws by Legislature Relating to Taxation in State Constitutions

Alabama	Art. IV, § 104 (15), (25), and (28)
Arizona	Art. IV, pt. 2, § 19, para. 9
California	Art. XIII, § 24
Colorado	Art. V, § 25; art. X, § 7
Florida	Art. III, § 11 (2) and (8)
Idaho	Art. III, § 19
Indiana	Art. IV, § 22
Iowa	Art. III, § 30
Kentucky	§ § 59 and 181
Louisiana	Art. III, § 12(A)(5)
Maryland	Art. III, § 33
Minnesota	Art. XII, § 1
Mississippi	Art. IV, § 90(h)
Missouri	Art. III, § 40 (7) and (8); art. X, § 10(a)
Nevada	Art. 4, § 20
New Jersey	Art. IV, § VII, para. 9(6)
New Mexico	Art. IV, § 24
New York	Art. III, §17
North Carolina	Art. II, § 24(1)(i) and (k)
North Dakota	Art. II, § 69
Oklahoma	Art. V, § 46; art. X, § 20
Oregon	Art. IV, § 23
Pennsylvania	Art. III, § 32(6)
South Dakota	Art. II, § 23(8)
Texas	Art. III, § 56
Utah	Art. XIII, § 5
Virginia	Art. IV, § 14
Washington	Art. II, § 28(5) and (14); art. XI, § 12
West Virginia	Art. VI, § 39
Wisconsin	Art. IV, § 31
Wyoming	Art. III, § 27

Table 11
Restrictions of State Taxation of Real Property

Arkansas	Amend. No. 47[a]
Hawaii	Art. VIII, § 3[b]
Nebraska	Art. VIII, § § 1A and 7[c]
Oklahoma	Art. X, § 9[a]
Texas	Art. VIII, § § la and le(1)[a]
Virginia	Art. X, § 4

[a]Restriction on ad valorem taxation.
[b]Restriction does not apply to County of Kalawao.
[c]Restriction relates to any property tax.

California introduced its own somewhat drastic version. All told, perhaps as many as seventy-five separate constitutional clauses of this nature were already in existence, applicable to the various taxing authorities of the states. So-called arithmetic limitations fall into a number of definable categories and subcategories. First, the limitation may refer more generally to state or local government revenues, or it may relate only to revenues from all property or, more specifically, revenues from real property. Second, a fixed percentage of taxation may be chosen, or a percentage of growth may be used instead. Sometimes an index such as consumer prices is substituted for percentage growth rates. The limitation may then be made applicable to the state, the local government (or a particular form of it), or both. Third, voting requirements (as for override) may be specified, either by referendum or legislative action, with a variety of suboptions possible. Table 16 lists the jurisdictions imposing arithmetic limitations in their constitutions, and the citations to the applicable provisions.

Requirements Relating to Tax Object or Purpose

A number of state constitutional provisions address themselves to the reason for the imposition of the power of taxation. These appear more or less in the form of three basic types. The first type simply requires that the "object of the tax" be stated in the act imposing it. The second type more or less specifically limits the purpose of a tax. The third type requires that a tax be used for "public purposes only". Table 17 sets forth the jurisdictions with constitutions containing clauses of this nature, with notation as to the type of clause in each case.

Dedication of Tax Revenue Requirements

Closely related to the preceding requirements in state constitutions, regarding the tax object or purpose, are those that require the dedication of the collected revenues. For the most part, it is probably best to consider this

Table 12
Municipal Charters and Home Rule Provisions in State Constitutions

Alaska	Art. X, § 11
Arizona	Art. XIII, § 2
Arkansas	Art. XII
California	Art. XI
Colorado	Art. XX, § § 4, 5, 6
Connecticut	Art. X
Florida	Art. VIII
Georgia	Art. IX
Hawaii	Art. VIII
Illinois	Art. VII, § 6
Iowa	Amend. 2 of 1968; amend. of 1978 to art. III
Kansas	Art. 12, § 5
Louisiana	Art. VI, § § 4, 5, 6, 8
Maine	Art. VIII, pt. II
Maryland	Art. XI-A, -E, -F
Massachusetts	Art. LXXXIX, arts. of amend.
Michigan	Art. VII, § § 2, 22
Minnesota	Art. XII
Missouri	Art. VI, § § 18 (a)-(l), 19-22, 30 (a)
Montana	Art. XI, § § 5, 6
Nebraska	Art. XI
Nevada	Art. 8, § 8
New Hampshire	Pt. I, art. 39
New Mexico	Art. X, § § 4, 5
New York	Art. IX
North Dakota	Art. VI
Ohio	Art. XVIII, § § 3, 7; art. X
Oklahoma	Art. XVIII, § 3(a)
Oregon	Art. VI, § 10; art. XI, § 2
Pennsylvania	Art. III, § 32; art. IX
Rhode Island	Art. XXVIII of amends.
South Carolina	Art. VIII, § 11
South Dakota	Art. IX, § 2
Tennessee	Art. XI, § 9
Texas	Art. XI, § § 4, 5
Utah	Art. XI, § 5
Virginia	Art. VII, § § 2, 3
Washington	Art. XI, § § 4, 10, 16
West Virginia	Art. VI, § 39 (a)
Wisconsin	Art. XI, § 3

kind of constraint as outside the scope of an investigation that is more concerned with regulatory considerations. It is no doubt a borderline situation. The most difficult constraint, of course, is that relating to the automobile and to highway construction, that is, the dedicated gas tax. There is no question that these measures can and have had a dramatic effect upon land and land development. However, it is felt that this may be more justifiably considered a spending question, in the sense of the kind of distinction that can be made between a tax and a program that taxes may directly or indirectly support, and, for the most part, is not within our scope.

Table 13

Territorial or Jurisdictional Limitations on Taxation in State Constitutions

Arizona	Art. IX, § 1[a]
Colorado	Art. X, §§ 3[a] and 10
Delaware	Art. VII, § 1[a]
Florida	Art. VII, § 2[a]; art. VIII, § 1(h)
Georgia	Art. VII, § I, para. III[a]
Idaho	Art. VII, § 5[a]
Kentucky	§ 171[a]
Missouri	Art. X, § 3[a]
Nebraska	Art. VIII, § 6[a]
New Mexico	Art. X, § 4(c)
North Carolina	Art. V, § 2(2)[a]
North Dakota	Art. XI, § 176[a]
Oregon	Art. I, § 32[a]
Pennsylvania	Art. VIII, § 1[a]
South Carolina	Art. X, § 6[a]
South Dakota	Art. XI, § 10[a]
Texas	Art. VIII, §§ 21(b), 23(a)
Virginia	Art. VII, § 2; art. X, § 1[a]
Washington	Art. VII, § 1[a] and 9[a]; art. XI, § 16
West Virginia	Art. X, § 9[a]

[a]Limitation is found in uniformity/equality clause, and relates thereto.

There is also a constitutional provision that works in the reverse way, that is, prohibiting the dedication of tax moneys, with stated exceptions. The State of Alaska has such a clause.

Table 18 sets forth the states having dedication-of-tax-revenue requirements in their constitutions, and the applicable citations to these provisions. Also, a separate listing indicates the provisions requiring highway earmarking of gasoline and related automobile taxes.

Special Voting or Approval Requirements
Relating to Taxation

In some states, where taxation is concerned, the constitution will require a special quorum or an extraordinary vote of the legislative bodies. There are also a number of other special voting requirements relating to taxation in state constitutions where the imposition or change in a tax is concerned. These have become an increasingly important constraint, and the kind of requirement imposed for increasing a tax is clearly demonstrated in the provisions of California's Proposition 13, where the previously discussed arithmetic limitation has been introduced in a drastic form. West Virginia, on the other hand, imposes a time limit of three years on tax increases authorized by referendum. Sometimes, state constitutions include a voting requirement where new legislative exemptions are to be added (e.g., South Carolina). A more basic requirement is also found in a number of constitu-

Table 14

Prohibitions against Delegation, Surrender, Suspension, or Contracting Away of the Taxing Power in State Constitutions

Alabama	Art. XI, § 212[a]
Alaska	Art. IX, § 1; art. X, § 2
Arizona	Art. IX, § 1[b]
Arkansas	Art. XVI, § 7[c]
California	Art. XI, § 11; art. XIII, § 31
Colorado	Art. V, § 35[a]; art. X, § 9[c]
Georgia	Art. VII, § I, para. I[b]
Hawaii	Art. VII, § 1[b]
Idaho	Art. VI, § 8[c]
Illinois	Art. IX, § 1[b]
Kentucky	§ 175[b]
Louisiana	Art. VII, pt. I, § 1[b]
Maine	Art. IX, § 9[b]
Michigan	Art. IX, § 2[b]
Minnesota	Art. X, § 1[b]
Mississippi	Art. VII, § 182[c]
Missouri	Art. X, § 2[b]
Montana	Art. VIII, § 2[b]
New York	Art. XVI, § 1[b]
North Carolina	Art. V, § 2(1) and 2(2)
North Dakota	Art. XI, § 178[b]
Oklahoma	Art. X, § 5[b]
Pennsylvania	Art. III, § 31[a]; art. VIII, § 6[c]
(Puerto Rico)	Art. VI, § 2[b]
South Dakota	Art. III, § 26; art. XI, § 3
Texas	Art. VIII, § 4[c]
Utah	Art. VI, § 28[a]
Virginia	Art. IV, § 15[c]
Washington	Art. VIII, § 1[b]
Wyoming	Art. III, § 37; art. XV, § 14

[a]Prohibition relates to nongovernmental delegation.

[b]Prohibition relates to surrender, suspension, or contracting away of the taxing power.

[c]Prohibition relates to surrender, suspension, or contracting away of the taxing power to private corporations.

tions, where "consent of the people" or their "representatives" is imposed upon taxing measures. Table 19 lists those states and the citation to the applicable constitutional provisions. It also contains the provisions relating to special quorums and extraordinary votes that are required in the legislative bodies of the states. Table 20 contains the constitutional citations to special voting requirements that have been mentioned.

"Grandfather" Provisions Relating to Taxation

A number of states have seen fit to protect or preserve certain interests or past practices by their constitutions. This is accomplished through a so-called "grandfather clause" preserving preexisting practices. Prominent among these is the clause preserving exemptions, found in seven of the states.

Another type preserves tax provisions where they exist in municipal charters. Table 21 sets forth the states having constitutional provisions of this nature, and the kind of tax provision that has been "grandfathered." There are also some provisions that preserve preconstitutional taxes.[40]

Table 15
Prohibitions against Impairment of the Obligation of Contracts in State Constitutions

Alabama	Art. I, § 22; art. IV, § 95
Alaska	Art. I, § 15[a]
Arizona	Art. II, § 25[a]
Arkansas	Art. II, § 17[b]
California	Art. I, § 9[a]
Colorado	Art. II, § 11[b]
Florida	D.Rts. art. I, § 10
Georgia	Art. I, § I, para. VII[a]
Idaho	Art. I, § 16[b]
Illinois	Art. I, § 16[a]
Indiana	Art. I, § 24
Iowa	Art. I, § 21
Kentucky	§ 19[a]
Louisiana	Art. I, § 23[a]
Maine	Art. I, § 11[a]
Michigan	Art. I, § 10[a]
Minnesota	Art. I, § 11[a]
Mississippi	Art. III, § 16[b]
Missouri	Art. I, § 13[a]
Montana	Art. II, § 31[a]
Nebraska	Art. I, § 16
Nevada	Art. 1, § 15
New Jersey	Art. IV, § VII, para. 3
New Mexico	Art. II, § 19
North Dakota	Art. I, § 16[a]
Ohio	Art. II, § 28
Oklahoma	Art. II, § 15[a]
Oregon	Art. I, § 21
Pennsylvania	Art. I, § 17[b]
(Puerto Rico)	Art. II, § 7[a]
Rhode Island	Art. I, § 12; art. XIV, § 2
South Carolina	Art. I, § 4
South Dakota	Art. VI, § 12[a]
Tennessee	Art. I, § 20; art. XI, § 2
Texas	Art. I, § 16[a]
Utah	Art. I, § 18
Virginia	Art. I, § 11[b]
Washington	Art. I, § 23[a]
West Virginia	Art. III, § 4
Wisconsin	Art. I, § 12
Wyoming	Art. I, § 35[a]

[a]Constitution also contains prohibition against contracting away of the taxing power. See table 14.
[b]Constitution also contains prohibition against contracting away of the taxing power to private corporations. See table 14.

Table 16
Arithmetic Limitations Relating to Taxation in State Constitutions

Alabama	Art. XI, § § 214, 216; amend. no. 111, § § 260, 269; amend. no. 3, art. XIX, § § 1, 2; amend. no. 25, art. XXII; amend. no. 56; amend. no. 202; amend. no. 208, § 215; amend. no. 212; amend. no. 373
Arkansas	Art. XII, § 4; art. XVI, § § 8, 9; amend. nos. 11, 18
California	Art. XIII, § § 2, 12, 21, 22; art. XIII A
Colorado	Art. X, § 11
Florida	Art. VII, § § 2, 5, 9
Georgia	Art. VII, § I, para. II; art. VIII, § VII, para. I
Idaho	Art. VII, § 9
Illinois	Art. IX, § § 3, 4
Kentucky	§ 157
Louisiana	Art. VI, pt. II, § § 26, 27, 28; art. VI, pt. III, § 39; art. VII, pt. I, § 4B; art. VII, pt. II, § 19; art. IX, § 8
Michigan	Art. VII, § 16; art. IX, § § 6, 8, 26, 31
Mississippi	Art. XI, § 236
Missouri	Art. X, § § 4(b), 8, 11(a), 11(b), 12(a)
Nebraska	Art. VIII, § 5
Nevada	Art. 10, § § 1, 2
New Mexico	Art. VIII, § 2
New York	Art. VIII, § 10
North Carolina	Art. V, § 2(6)
North Dakota	Art. XI, § 174
Ohio	Art. XII, § 2; art. XVIII, § 11
Oklahoma	Art. X, § § 8, 9
Oregon	Art. XI, § 11
South Dakota	Art. XI, § 1
Texas	Art. VIII, § § 1, 9; art. XI, § § 4, 5
Utah	Art. XIII, § § 3, 7
Washington	Art. VII, § 2
West Virginia	Art. X, § § 1, 7
Wyoming	Art. XV, § § 4, 5, and 6

Prohibitions against Discriminatory Taxation
of Nonresidents

A number of states have specific provisions in their constitutions against discriminatory taxation of nonresidents. Several of these appeared quite early historically, having been introduced by virtue of the original organic acts relating to the establishment of statehood. These provisions may currently become more important, particularly where "growth policy" (or exclusionary!) efforts come to be involved. Current attempts to control second-home development and antispeculation measures through taxation would notably be vulnerable to state constitutional constraints of this kind. As a matter of fact, these considerations would also tend to overlap with the federal "right-to-travel" doctrine that has been evolving under the Fourteenth Amendment to the U.S. Constitution (and, to a certain extent, the

Table 17
Requirements Relating to Tax Object or Purpose in State Constitutions

Alaska	Art. IX, § 6[a]
Arizona	Art. IX, § 1[a] and §§ 3 and 9[b]
Arkansas	Art. V, § 31; art. XVI, § 11[b]; amend. no. 18
Florida	Art. VIII, § 1(h)
Georgia	Art. VII, § I, para. III[a], and § II, para. I; art. IX, § IV, para. II and III, and § V[a]
Hawaii	Art. VII, § 4[a]
Iowa	Art. VII, § 7[b]
Kansas	Art. 7, § 5; art. 11, § 5[b]
Kentucky	§§ 171[a] and 180[b]
Louisiana	Art. VI, pt. II, § 30[a]; art. VII, pt. I, § 1[a]
Michigan	Art. VII, § 21[a]
Minnesota	Art. X, § 1[a]
Missouri	Art. X, §§ 1 and 3[a]
Montana	Art. VIII, § 1[a]
New York	Art. III, § 22[b]
North Carolina	Art. V, §§ 2[a] and 5[b]
North Dakota	Art. VI, § 130; art. XI, § 175[b]
Ohio	Art. XII, § 5[b]
Oklahoma	Art. X, §§ 9, 14[a], and 19[b]
Oregon	Art. IX, § 3[b]
South Carolina	Art. X, § 5[a]
South Dakota	Art. XI, §§ 2[a] and 8[b]
Tennessee	Art. II, § 28[a]
Texas	Art. VIII, § 3[a]
Washington	Art. VII, §§ 1[a] and 5[b]
Wyoming	Art. XIII, § 3[a]; art. XV, § 13[b]

Note: The listing of clauses restricting the purposes of taxation herein is not intended to include within its scope those providing for *special purpose taxes*, as for public schools.

[a]Specifically requires taxation to be for "public purposes" only.

[b]Requires that taxation have a stated object or purpose.

commerce clause, art. I, §8, cl. 3). There may also be overlapping with the federal privileges and immunities clause of art. IV, §2, cl. 1. See chapter 5, note 71. Where both state and federal clauses are involved, their interaction must be considered. Table 22 sets forth the states having constitutions containing prohibitions against discriminatory taxation of nonresidents, and the pertinent citations thereto.

Prohibitions against Duplicate Taxation

Finally, a few states specifically provide against certain kinds of duplicate taxation. These provisions vary broadly, with prohibition against taxation on property for the same purpose within the same year, with individual and corporate income taxes, with a severance tax as the only tax on timber, and with intangibles not being subject to both property and income taxes. Table 23 sets forth the states having prohibitions of this nature in their constitutions, with citation to the applicable provisions and notation of the constraints involved.

Note on the Structure of Exemptions in State Constitutional Law

For our purposes, it is probably most convenient to consider the subject of exemptions—allowing and prohibiting them—as encompassing other related provisions of varying magnitude, such as extensions, exceptions, forgiveness, or abatements. At the state constitutional level, the structure may be summarized as follows: If there is a uniformity and equality clause, exemptions may be prohibited unless there are classification-related clause provisions that permit it generally, or specific exemption clauses that do so elsewhere in the constitution. If there are no provisions one way or the other, exemptions

Table 18
Dedication-of-Tax-Revenue Requirements

Alaska	Art. IX, § § 7[a] and 15
California	Art. XVI, § 16[b]
Louisiana	Art. IX, § 9
Missouri	Amend. 1976, art. IV, § 43(a); art. X, § 12(a)
Montana	Art. IX, § 5
New Jersey	Art. VIII, § 1, para. 7
New Mexico	Amend. art. VIII
North Dakota	Art. XI, § 177
Texas	Art. VIII, § 1-a
Wyoming	Art. XV, § 18
Gasoline Taxes—Highway Earmarking	
Alabama	Amend. no. 354 of amend. no. 93
Arizona	Art. IX, § 14
California	Art. XIX
Colorado	Art. X, § 18
Florida	Art. XII, § 9(c)
Idaho	Art. VII, § 17
Maine	Art. IX, § 19
Massachusetts	Amend. art. CIV of art. LXXVIII
Michigan	Art. IX, § 9
Minnesota	Art. XIV
Missouri	Art. IV, § 30
Montana	Art. VIII, § 6
New Hampshire	Pt. II, art. 6-a
North Dakota	Amend. art. 56
Ohio	Art. XII, § 5a
Oregon	Art. IX, § 3
Pennsylvania	Art. VIII, § 11
South Dakota	Art. XI, § 8
Texas	Art. VIII, § 7a
Utah	Art. XIII, § 13
Washington	Art. II, § 40
West Virginia	Art. VI, § 52
Wyoming	Art. 15, § 16

[a]General prohibition against dedication of tax revenues, with stated exceptions.
[b]Enabling provision for redevelopment projects.

Table 19
Consent of People or Representatives Requirements Relating to Taxation in State Constitutions

Maine	Art. I, § 22
Maryland	D.Rts. art. 14
Massachusetts	D.Rts. pt. I, art. 23
New Hampshire	Pt. I, art. 28
North Carolina	Art. I, § 8
Oregon	Art. I, § 32
South Carolina	Art. X, § 5
South Dakota	Art. VI, § 17
Texas	Art. VIII, § 10
Virginia	Art. I, § 6
Wyoming	Art. I, § 28

Special-Legislative-Quorum Requirements

New York	Art. III, § 23 (3/5 each house)
Vermont	Art. II, § 14 (2/3 each house)
Wisconsin	Art. VIII, § 8 (3/5 each house)

Special-Legislative-Majority Requirements

Arkansas	Art. V, § 31 (2/3 both houses)
Louisiana	Art. VII, pt. I, § 2 (2/3 both houses)
Mississippi	Art. IV, § 70 (3/5 both houses)
Virginia	Art. IV, § 11 (majority all members both houses)

Table 20
Special Voting Requirements Relating to Taxation in State Constitutions

Alabama	Amend. no. 3, art. XIX; amend. no. 56; amend. no. 111, § 269; amend. no. 202; amend. no. 373
Arkansas	Art. V, § 31; art. XIX, § 27; amend. nos. 18 and 19
California	Art. XI, § 14; art. XIII A, § § 3 and 4
Florida	Art. VII, § 5
Hawaii	Art. XVIII, § 6
Idaho	Art. VII, § 9
Illinois	Art. VII, § 6(g)
Kentucky	§ 171
Louisiana	Art. VI, pt. II, § 32
Michigan	Art. IX, § § 6, 25, 26, 27, 31
Mississippi	Art. IV, § 70
Missouri	Art. X, § 12(a)
New Mexico	Art. VIII, § 2
North Carolina	Art. V, § 2(5)
Oklahoma	Art. X, § 6
South Carolina	Art. X, § § 2(d) and 3
South Dakota	Art. XI
Texas	Art. VIII, § 10
Utah	Art. XIV, § 8
Virginia	Art. X, § 6(6)
Washington	Art. VII, § 2(a)
West Virginia	Art. X, § 1

would be permitted by statute. Also, the last two "lax" *effective*-uniformity interpretations that were discussed in the first part of this chapter (Classes 6 and 7, see table 2) would similarly permit free *statutory* exemption if specific exemptions did not already exist in the particular constitution in question.

Where they are specifically provided for in state constitutions, exemptions fall into some very definite clusters of subjects. The following is an overview of the principal exempt categories:

1. Whether or not it is necessary, all the various levels of government are seen as specified: federal, state, county, municipal, school, or special-purpose districts.

2. The next group encompasses religious and humanistic uses and ownership generally, and is most often specified as churches, hospitals, cemeteries, charities, and educational, cultural, and scientific institutions and libraries.

3. Another group specifies certain disadvantaged taxpayers, most usually widows, the elderly, and the disabled (principally veterans).

4. The homestead exemption is an old and widespread institution, taking a number of different forms.

5. There are a number of special-interest exemptions (functioning, perhaps, in the "grey area" of public interest), particularly banks, labor organizations, industry (usually new industry), and veterans', fraternal, and patriotic organizations.

6. Certain kinds of facilities that are presumably "cloaked with a public interest" have also been singled out, such as wharves, waterways, canals, levees, reservoirs, and irrigation facilities.

7. A large new category has been added recently, relating to conservation and environmental concerns. These appear in the form of pollution and solar energy facilities, open space, recreation, agriculture, forest and historic preservation, and urban-renewal projects.

8. In some cases, certain interests in real property may be permitted exemption. These have included leasehold interests and rights-of-way.

9. Finally, some constitutions have simply included a provision allowing the exemption of "public uses," while others may call for "strict construction" of the specified exemptions permitted.

Note on the Scope of State Taxes and Taxable Objects and Events Considered

Some attention should be given at this point to the particular taxes and the particular taxable objects or events that are governed by existing state constitutional constraints. There are, in fact, several other considerations, in addition to the basic ad valorem tax on land. Actually, taxation of all property is important in the sense not just of improvements, but of intangible and personal property interests as well—in the form of mortgages, choses, or other paper interests, on the one hand, and mobile homes, on the other; certainly these, too, may have important effects upon land and real property generally.

The foremost tax of our time is, of course, the tax upon income. This tax does not exist in all states, although it does not appear to be unequivocally prohibited in any. New Jersey requires that any income tax imposed be used for reducing property taxes. Wyoming has a similar provision relating to crediting to a broader range of other taxes. Alabama, Florida, North Carolina, and Utah impose a percentage limitation on any income tax. And Illinois and Michigan specifically prohibit graduated or progressive rates of taxation. There also arises the interesting question, already mentioned, of whether income is to be considered property for purposes of uniformity and equality. Where this is the case, a constitutional amendment may be necessary to allow such form of income taxation.

The following is a summary of the other most important categories of taxes that may come into play here:

1. Taxes on estates and inheritances;
2. Sales, transaction, and stamp taxes;
3. Privilege, license, franchise, and occupation taxes;
4. Severance taxes (such as on timber) and related taxes on mining, ores, mineral, gas, oil, and the like;
5. Other excise taxes;
6. Special assessments.

It must be remembered that each of these categories has significantly different characteristics that enable it to be distinguished in terms of the

Table 21
Grandfather Provisions Relating to Taxation in State Constitutions

Alabama	Amend. 373 (exemptions)
Alaska	Art. IX, § 7 (dedicated tax revenues)
Hawaii	Art. XVIII, § 6 (exemptions)
Idaho	Art. VII, § 5 (exemptions)
Mississippi	Art. VII, § 181 (corporate exemptions)
New Jersey	Art. VIII, § 1, para. 2 (exemptions)
North Dakota	Art. XI, § 176 (general provision)
Oklahoma	Art. X, § 6 (treaty exemptions)
Pennsylvania	Art. VIII, § 4 (public utility taxation)
South Carolina	Art. X, § 2(c)[a] and 3[b]
Tennessee	Art. XI, § 9 (municipal charter provisions)
Virginia	Art. X, § 6(f) (exemptions)
Washington	Art. VI, § 2 (port or utility-district rates)

[a]Continues method of ad valorem assessment.

[b]Repeals exemptions not specifically provided for on March 1, 1978.

Table 22
Prohibitions against Discriminatory Taxation of Nonresidents in State Constitutions

Alaska	Art. IX, § 2
Arizona	Art. XX, § 5
Idaho	Art. XXI, § 19
Missouri	Art. III, § 43
Montana	Ord. I(2) and § 4, Second of Enabling Act
Nevada	Ord. Third
New Mexico	Art. XXI, § 2
North Dakota	Art. XVI, § 203(2)
Oklahoma	Art. I, § 3
South Dakota	Art. XXII, § 2; art. XXVI, § 18(2)
Utah	Art. III, § 2
Washington	Art. XXVI, § 2
Wisconsin	Art. II, § 2
Wyoming	Art. XXI, § 26

applicability of constitutional constraints. Intimately related to this is the question of whether there is a *police power* or *tax* basis involved.

Other important subjects of taxation might include: (1) railroads and other transportation facilities and (2) utilities.

Note on Provisions Relating Principally to the Mechanics of Arriving at a Tax

Another important area of constraint deals with what are essentially the mechanics of arriving at a tax. This would include: (1) whether or not land and improvements are to be valued or assessed separately or together; (2) how classification may be applied—for example, real property may be required to constitute a single or minimum class; or (3) provisions outlining and prescribing valuation or assessment formulas in some detail, or restricting or limiting valuation or assessment practices.

Table 23
Prohibitions against Duplicate Taxation in State Constitutions

Idaho	Art. VII, § 5 (on property for same purpose within same year)
Illinois	Art. IX, § 3 (individual and corporate income taxes)
Louisiana	Art. VII, pt. I, § 4(B) (severance tax as only tax on timber)
Utah	Art. XIII, § 3 (intangibles not subject to both property and income taxes)

Other Constraints

A new requirement that is sure to grow in importance in the future is that providing for notice and public hearings where taxes are to be increased. Such a provision appeared in the November 1978 amendment to the Texas Constitution.[41]

There are, finally, the partial or outright prohibitions against certain types of taxes by various taxing agencies. Perhaps the most interesting of these is Ohio's "Anti-George" clause (Henry George, that is), which reads, in part: "The powers defined herein as the "initiative" and "referendum" shall not be used to pass a law . . . authorizing the levy of any single tax on land values or land sites at a higher rate or by a different rule than is or may be applied to improvements thereon. . . ."[42]

Conclusion

The foregoing analysis does not purport to be exhaustive of each and every constitutional provision that may operate as a constraint upon the taxing power as an instrument of land-planning policy. However, the provisions discussed do represent the more significant clusters that indicate potentially conflicting policy considerations of more than an isolated nature at the state constitutional level.

Since comprehensive regulatory taxation where land is concerned has, for the most part, remained untried, it is not predictable what interpretive law may develop from the many existing provisions in state constitutions setting forth potential constraints. The scope of the uniformity-and-equality clause analysis represented by the Newhouse study, discussed herein, indicates the magnitude of legal interpretive considerations that can come to be involved.

Yet the difficulty of the task of tax reform is as nothing compared to the economic and political havoc that can be visited upon us by a system that is unresponsive and insensitive to our broader values. A subsequent portion of this study will attempt to deal more fully with these questions and issues on the basis of policy analysis and case studies.

Notes

1. *Supra* p. 10.

2. The Connecticut Constitution is instructive in this regard, with its total absence of tax provisions. Notwithstanding, in that state there are some two dozen kinds of taxes currently in effect.

3. See *supra*, p. 10.

4. Bernard, *Constitutions, Taxation, and Land Policy* (1979).

5. Newhouse, *Constitutional Uniformity and Equality in State Taxation* (U. of Michigan, Michigan Legal Studies, 1959).

6. The Newhouse definition here is as follows: "If all property must be selected, and no property may be exempted, there is said to be a requirement of universality." *Supra* note 5, at 7.

7. The effective rate is the combined base-rate structure.

8. The eighth mathematical choice was evidently discarded, since it would read: "Universality/absolute uniformity in effective rates/ NO AD VALOREM REQUIREMENT."

9. It is interesting to note that implicit in the ranking of the Newhouse evaluation was a value assignment system ranging from -1 to -4 (the negative value introducing more laxity from the strictest combination, which would include all three factors) and consisting of the following assignments (see table 2): (a) $= -2$; (b) $= -4$; (c) $= -1$. See Newhouse, *supra* note 5, at 675.

10. Historically speaking, there was a time when state constitutions did not, for the most part, contain provisions that required uniformity in taxation (1789-1818). These were later added during a "restrictive" period (1818-1896). In 1874, Pennsylvania introduced the first true classification modifier (for phraseology, see table 1, Type VII). In 1911, another liberal classification clause was introduced (table 1, Type VIII), and in 1913, the practice of adding supplementary or alternative clauses providing for special treatment of enumerated classes of property notwithstanding the continued presence of an original strict uniformity clause. There are now forty-six constitutions that have some kind of uniformity/equality provision and twenty-three constitutions that have specific classification-enabling provisions of some kind. Five jurisdictions have no uniformity/equality provisions at all, and two have provisions so weak as to leave a total of seven jurisdictions that were left free to classify, from a state constitutional standpoint. Thus, thirty states may classify in some sense. It should be noted, however, that there is a distinct difference between what has been constitutionally enabled, or left unimpeded, and what has been implemented. See Newhouse, *supra* note 5, at 610-642.

11. Newhouse, *supra* note 5, at 4.

12. See Newhouse, *supra* note 5, at 609 (chapter V, entitled "A Comparative Analysis of the Uniformity Limitations").

13. As indicated, these are prototypical, and some variation in phrasing from state to state will be found. Where new constitutions have been enacted since the date of the Newhouse study, this has been noted as "changed" in the Table. Where only a new clause has been substituted, the notation "new clause" is found. Where the basic clause is retained but another added, the notation "clause added" is found.

14. Responsibility for this table, therefore, is the editor's. Although constitutional documents are considered to be rather "stable" as laws go, it must be observed that enough change takes place here, too, to make regular periodic updating necessary and attempts at definitive classification difficult.

15. See Newhouse, *supra* note 5, at 677-678.

16. Entries for the states that have since changed their constitutions substantially have been omitted (see table 3B for new provisions). No entry was made for the State of Louisiana in the original table; consequently, this, too, has been deleted. Two additional states, Georgia and North Carolina, appear to have been entered incorrectly on the original table by typographical error(?). Cf. Newhouse, *id*. at 679.

17. *Supra* note 5, at 683.

18. *Id*. at 647-648.

19. *Id*. at 688.

20. *Id*.

21. *Id*.

22. ". . . [T]he complex historical growth of the uniformity provisions . . . emphasizes the danger of referring to 'the' requirement of uniformity and equality found in state constitutions, for such a reference is latent with potentially misleading conclusions. . . . Although having identical clauses, different results will often be dictated by supplementary provisions which are often ignored by writers when classifying the several states as to their types of uniformity limitations." Newhouse, *supra* note 5, at 643, 663.

23. For example, the question of whether a tax may be "graduated" may depend upon the determination of whether "income" is considered to be "property" within the meaning of the taxation provisions. *Id*. at 646, 666, 688. Whether or not it is considered to be a tax on property, the income tax possesses powerful potential as a land regulator.

24. We should not limit our inquiry to tangible property, or real property, since mortgage interests, for example, may be an important potential subject for regulatory taxation affecting land.

25. For example, property, sales, income.

26. The effective rate of a property tax is the combined base-rate structure. This combination is significant because property selected for property taxation may be classified for the application of different effective rates in either of two ways. First, all property may be assessed for taxation at the same ratio of valuation and different percentage rates applied to different classes of property. The ratio of valuation is the percentage of "actual" value at which property is entered on the tax rolls. Second, all property may be subject to the same percentage rate but classified for the application of different ratios of valuation. (The state-by-state analysis in-

dicated that, regardless of the strictness of the uniformity limitation applicable to the effective rate, there was no prohibition against classification of property for the purpose of reaching a figure to be used as the "value" of the property.) Note, also, that the uniformity limitation is a *territorial* requirement. That is, rates imposed by the state must be uniform throughout the state, those by the county throughout the county, and so forth. There is no requirement that the rates of different taxing authorities be correlated. Newhouse, *supra* note 5, at 7, 667.

27. For example, ad valorem or non-ad valorem ("specific") taxes. (The latter may be contained in a separate uniformity clause. See *supra* note 5, at 646.)

28. However, property may be considered a "minimum class". See *supra* note 5, at 657, 661-663. This relates in particular to the consideration of (b) rates of taxation.

29. Although classification for rates was found to be possible in about half the states, not every state that apparently can utilize classification for rates has done so. See *supra* note 5, at 664.

30. Newhouse, *supra* note 5, at 595.

31. In *Bell's Gap R.R. Co. v. Pennsylvania*, 134 U.S. 232 (1890), the U.S. Supreme Court established the applicability, in principle, of the equal-protection clause as a limitation upon state tax legislation. See also *Walters v. City of St. Louis*, 347 U.S. 231, 237 (1954), and Scholley, *Equal Protection in Tax Legislation*, 24 Va. L. Rev. 229 and 388 (1938); Newhouse, *supra* note 5, at 601-608.

32. Property may be classified as realty and personalty, tangible and intangible. *Bell's Gap R.R. Co. v. Pennsylvania, supra* note 31. Subclassification of intangibles was permitted in *Klein v. Board of Supervisors*, 282 U.S. 19 (1930); tangibles, *Heisler v. Thomas Colliery Co., supra* chapter 5, note 58. Railroad property was permitted as a classification as distinct from all other property: cases cited and discussed in Sholley, *supra* note 31. Progressivity was upheld in *Magoun v. Illinois Trust and Savings*, 170 U.S. 283 (1898), where graduated rates on the Illinois inheritance tax were involved, and in *Shaffer v. Carter*, 252 U.S. 37 (1920), where the graduated income tax was reviewed. Also upheld was a graduated license tax on theaters according to admission price in *Metropolis Theatre Co. v. Chicago*, 228 U.S. 61 (1913). See also reference to the *Grosjean* and *Jackson* line of cases, *supra* chapter 5, notes 84, 100, and 101. The upper limit was reached in the *Hillsborough* case, *supra* chapter 5, note 108, where the court indicated that the consistent, systematic, and intentional discrimination in the assessment of a taxpayer's property for the purposes of ad valorem taxation would be invalid. Another case, of perhaps doubtful current vitality, is *Louisville Gas & Electric Co. v. Coleman, supra* chapter 5, note 101, holding invalid a tax on the recording of mortgages of less than five years' maturity.

33. *Supra* note 5, at 608. See also table 6 herein.

34. *Supra* note 5, at 601-608.

35. It has thus been suggested that the elimination of the disparate individual sets of uniformity clauses that are to be found in state constitutions would result in the establishment of a fairly consistent and liberal constitutional standard of uniformity under federal and state equal-protection provisions. See Mathews, *The Function of Constitutional Provisions Requiring Uniformity in Taxation*, 38 Ky. L. J. 31, 187, 377 and 503 (1950).

36. D. Rts. pt. I, art. 6.

37. *Supra* page 10, and chapter 2, note 48.

38. These relate to assessment, levy, collection, exemptions, extensions, releases, remissions, and the tax purposes themselves, among other things.

39. Assuming that contracts of this nature ordinarily would not have been made with individuals. Otherwise, the effective total would be twenty-two.

40. See Louisiana Constitution, art. VII, pt. II, §22.

41. Texas Constitution, art. VIII, §21.

42. Ohio Constitution, art. II, §1(e).

Selected Cited References

Books

American Law Institute/American Bar Association. *Course of Study Materials on Taxation as a Land Use Control* (1979).

Bernard, Michael M. *Constitutions, Taxation, and Land Policy—Abstracts of Federal and State Constitutional Constraints on the Power of Taxation Relating to Land-Planning Policy* (Lexington, Mass.: Lexington Books, D.C. Heath, 1979).

Bureau of Internal Revenue. *History of the Internal Revenue Service 1791-1929* (U.S. Government Printing Office, 1930).

Cooley, Thomas McIntyre. *Taxation* (2nd ed.) (Chicago: Callaghan, 1886).

Commons, John R. *Institutional Economics* (1934) (University of Wisconsin Reprint, 2 vols., 1964).

Congressional Research Service, Library of Congress. *The Constitution of the United States of America* (U.S. Government Printing Office, 1973).

Corwin, Edward S. *The Constitution* (14th ed.) (Princeton: Princeton University Press, 1978; also 13th ed., 1973).

Cushman, Robert F. *Constitutional Law* (5th ed.) (Englewood Cliffs, N.J.: Prentice-Hall, 1979).

Elliot, Jonathan. *Debates on the Adoption of the Federal Constitution in the Convention Held at Philadelphia in 1787; With a Diary of the Debates of the Congress of the Confederation; As Reported by James Madison, a Member and Deputy From Virginia* (1845).

Griswold, Erwin N. *Federal Taxation* (6th ed.) (Brooklyn: Foundation Press, 1966).

(Hamilton, Alexander). *The Federalist*, Nos. 30-36 (taxation) (ca. 1787-88).

Newhouse, Wade J. *Constitutional Uniformity and Equality in State Taxation* (University of Michigan, Michigan Legal Studies, 1959).

Paul, Randolph E. *Taxation in the United States* (Boston: Little, Brown, 1954).

Ratner, Sidney. *American Taxation* (New York: W.W. Norton, 1942).

Seligman, Edwin R.A. *The Income Tax* (2nd ed.) (New York: Macmillan, 1914; Augustus M. Kelley Reprint, 1970).

Seligman, Edwin R.A. *Essays in Taxation* (10th ed.) (New York: Macmillan, 1931; Augustus M. Kelley Reprint, 1969).

Shurtleff & Olmsted. *Carrying Out the City Plan—The Practical Application of American Law in the Execution of City Plans* (New York: Russell Sage, 1914).

Story, Joseph. *Commentaries on the Constitution of the United States* (1833) (5th ed.) (Boston: Little, Brown, 1905).

Surrey and Warren. *Federal Income Taxation* (Brooklyn: Foundation Press, 1962).

Journals

Bernard, Michael M. *The Development of a Body of City Planning Law,* 51 American Bar Association Journal 632 (July 1965).

Bernard, Michael M. *The Comprehensive Plan Concept as a Basis for Legal Reform*, 44 University of Detroit Journal of Urban Law 611 (1967).

Bullock, Charles J. *The Origin, Purpose and Effect of the Direct Tax Clause of the Federal Constitution*, 15 Political Science Quarterly 217 and 452 (1900).

Cushman, Robert E. *The National Police Power Under the Commerce Clause of the Constitution*, 3 Minnesota Law Review 289, 381, 452 (1919).

Cushman, Robert E. *The National Police Power Under the Taxing Clause of the Constitution*, 4 Minnesota Law Review 247 (1920).

Cushman, Robert E. *Social and Economic Control Through Federal Taxation*, 18 Minnesota Law Review 759 (1934).

Gunter, Gerald. *Foreword: In Search of Evolving Doctrine on a Changing Court: A Model for a Newer Equal Protection*, 86 Harvard Law Review 1 (1972).

Mathews, William L. *The Function of Constitutional Provisions Requiring Uniformity in Taxation*, 38 Kentucky Law Journal 31, 187, 377 and 503 (1950).

Scholley, John B. *Equal Protection in Tax Legislation*, 24 Virginia Law Review 229 and 388 (1938).

Symposium: Future Directions for School Finance Reform, 38 Law & Contemporary Problems, No. 3 (Winter-Spring 1974).

Zimmerman, Edward A. *Tax Planning for Land Use Control*, 5 Urban Lawyer 639 (1973).

Table of Cases

Table of U.S. Constitutional Provisions

113

Addendum to the First Volume

United States Constitution

Art. IV., §2. [cl. 1.] The Citizens of each State shall be entitled to all Privileges and Immunities of Citizens in the several States.

Alabama Constitution

Art. IV, §104. The legislature shall not pass a special, private, or local law in any of the following cases:

. . . .

(15) Regulating either the assessment or collection of taxes. . . .

. . . .

(25) Exempting property from taxation or from levy or sale;

. . . .

(28) Remitting fines, penalties, or forfeitures;

. . . .

Amend. No. 373. Art. XI, §217. **Classification of taxable property for purposes of ad valorem taxation; taxable property to be taxed by state, counties, municipalities, etc., at same rate; assessment ratios for purposes of ad valorem taxation; increase or decrease of assessment ratios by counties, municipalities, etc.; increase or decrease of ad valorem tax rates by counties, municipalities, etc.; maximum amount of ad valorem tax; certain property to be assessed at current use value and not market value; exemption of certain property from ad valorem taxation; interpretation of authority for counties, municipalities, etc., to levy taxes, borrow money, etc., in relation to assessment of property; counties, municipalities, etc., authorized to levy additional ad valorem tax for costs of certain state-wide reappraisal of property.**

(a) On and after October 1, 1978, all taxable property within this state, not exempt by law, shall be divided into the following classes for the purposes of ad valorem taxation:

Class I. All property of utilities used in the business of such utilities.

Class II. All property not otherwise classified.

Class III. All agricultural, forest and single-family owner-occupied residential property, and historic buildings and sites.

Class IV. All private passenger automobiles and motor trucks of the type commonly known as "pickups" or "pickup trucks" owned and operated by an individual for personal or private use and not for hire, rent or compensation.

(b) With respect to ad valorem taxes levied by the state, all taxable property shall be forever taxed at the same rate. On and after October 1, 1978, such property shall be assessed for ad valorem tax purposes according to the classes thereof as herein defined at the following ratios of assessed value to the fair and reasonable market value (except as otherwise provided in subsection (j) hereof) of such property:

Class I. 30 per centum.
Class II. 20 per centum.
Class III. 10 per centum.
Class IV. 15 per centum.

(c) With respect to ad valorem taxes levied by counties, municipalities or other taxing authorities, all taxable property shall be forever taxed at the same rate. On and after October 1, 1978, such property shall be assessed for ad valorem tax purposes according to the classes of property defined in subsection (a) hereof and at the same ratios of assessed value to the fair and reasonable market value thereof as fixed in subsection (b) hereof, except as otherwise provided in subsection (j) hereof and this subsection (such ratios being herein called "assessment ratios"). In connection with the ad valorem taxes that a county, municipality or other taxing authority is authorized or required to levy and collect pursuant to any provision of this Constitution, for the ad valorem tax year beginning October 1, 1978, any such taxing authority may, subject to criteria established by act of the legislature, by resolution of the governing body of that taxing authority, at any time not later than September 30, 1979, increase or decrease the assessment ratio applicable to any class of taxable property, such increase or decrease to be effective for ad valorem tax years beginning on and after October 1, 1978. If (1) a county, municipality or other taxing authority adjusts an assessment ratio pursuant to the preceding sentence and (2) the receipts from all ad valorem taxes levied by or with respect to such taxing authority during the ad valorem tax year beginning October 1, 1978, exceed by more than five percent, or are less than 95 percent of, the receipts from such ad valorem taxes for the ad valorem tax year beginning October 1, 1977, then at any time not later than September 30, 1980, for ad valorem tax years beginning on and after October 1, 1979, the taxing authority may, subject to criteria established by act of the legislature, by resolution of the governing body of that taxing authority, adjust any assessment ratio applicable to any class of taxable property. On and after October 1, 1979, the governing body of any county, municipality or other taxing authority may, subject to criteria established by act of the legislature, at any time increase or decrease the assessment ratio applicable to any class of taxable property; provided, that any proposed adjustment to an assessment ratio to be made pursuant to this sentence, whether an increase or a decrease, shall have been (1) proposed by the governing body of the taxing authority after a public hearing on such proposal, (2) thereafter approved by an act of the legislature, and (3) subsequently approved by a majority vote of the qualified electors residing in the taxing authority who vote on the proposal at a special election called and held in accordance with the law governing special elections. No decrease in an assessment ratio pursuant to this subsection (c) shall be permitted with respect to either of the ad valorem tax years beginning October 1, 1978, and October 1, 1979, if such county, municipality or other taxing authority has increased any millage rate under subsection (e) of this section with respect to such ad valorem tax year. The legislature shall enact general laws applicable to all counties, municipalities and other taxing authorities regulating and establishing criteria for the exercise of the powers granted such taxing authorities to adjust assessment ratios as hereinabove provided. Such assessment ratios as herein authorized may vary among taxing authorities so long as each such assessment ratio is uniform within a taxing authority. Any decrease in any assessment ratio pursuant to this subsection shall not jeopardize the payment of any bonded indebtedness secured by any tax levied by the taxing authority decreasing the assessment ratio. Any action authorized by this subsection to be taken by a taxing authority, or the governing body thereof, shall, other than in the case of a municipality, be taken by resolution of the governing body of the county in which such taxing authority is located acting on behalf of such taxing authority.

(d) With respect to ad valorem taxes levied by the state or by any county, municipality or other taxing authority, no class of taxable property shall have an assessment ratio of less than five per centum nor more than 35 per centum.

(e) A county, municipality or other taxing authority may decrease any ad valorem tax rate at any time, provided such decrease shall not jeopardize the payment of any bonded indebtedness secured by such tax. For the ad valorem tax year beginning October 1, 1978, when the tax assessor of each county shall complete the assembly of the assessment book for his county for that ad valorem tax year and the computation of ad valorem taxes that will be paid upon such assessment, he shall certify to each authority within his county that levies an ad valorem tax the amount of ad valorem tax that will be produced by every levy in that ad valorem tax year but excluding for this purpose any assessment of new taxable property not previously subject to taxation (except "escaped" property as defined by law) added to the tax rolls of such county for the ad valorem tax year in which such certification is made that was not included on the tax rolls for the next preceding ad valorem tax year. Any county, municipality or other taxing authority, at any time not later than September 30, 1979, may increase the rate at which any ad valorem tax is levied by or with respect to that taxing authority above the limit otherwise provided in this Constitution, provided that the amount of the above-described certification of anticipated tax receipts with respect to such tax is less than 120 percent of the actual receipts from such tax for the ad valorem tax year beginning October 1, 1977, such increase to be effective for ad valorem tax years beginning on and after October 1, 1978; provided, that any such millage increase shall not exceed in mills the total of (i) the number of additional mills that is necessary, when added to the millage rate imposed with respect to such tax on each dollar of taxable property situated in the taxing authority for the ad valorem tax year beginning October 1, 1977, to produce revenue that is not less than and that is substantially equal to that received by the taxing authority with respect to such tax during such immediately preceding ad valorem tax year, plus (ii) a number of additional mills equal to 20 percent of the total mills imposed by that taxing authority with respect to such tax on each dollar of taxable property situated in the taxing authority for the ad valorem tax year beginning October 1, 1977. If, for the ad valorem tax year beginning October 1, 1978, the receipts from any ad valorem tax with respect to which any millage rate has been increased pursuant to the immediately preceding sentence are less than 95 percent of the receipts from such ad valorem tax for the ad valorem tax year beginning October 1, 1977, then at any time not later than September 30, 1980, the taxing authority may increase any millage rate with respect to such ad valorem tax in the manner provided in the immediately preceding sentence, such increase to be effective for ad valorem tax years beginning on and after October 1, 1979. It is further provided that all millage adjustments shall be made in increments of not less than one tenth (1/10) mill.

(f) On and after October 1, 1979, any county, municipality or other taxing authority may at any time increase the rate at which any ad valorem tax is levied above the limit otherwise provided in this Constitution; provided, that the proposed increase to be made pursuant to this subsection shall have been (1) proposed by the governing body of the taxing authority after a public hearing on such proposal, (2) thereafter approved by an act of the legislature, and (3) subsequently approved by a majority vote of the qualified electors residing in the taxing authority who vote on the proposal at a special election called and held in accordance with the law governing special elections. Any adjustments or other actions authorized to be made or taken pursuant to this subsection and subsection (e) hereof shall be made or taken by resolution of the governing body of such taxing authority, or if there is no such governing body and in the case of a taxing authority other than a municipality, by resolution of the governing body of the county in which such taxing authority is located acting on behalf of such taxing authority. The provisions of subsections (c), (e) and (f) of this section shall not apply to ad valorem taxes levied by the state.

(g) The legislature is authorized to enact legislation to implement the provisions of this section and may provide for exemptions from taxation; provided, that unless otherwise expressly provided, no amendment to this section shall be construed to repeal any statutory exemption existing on the effective date of any such amendment hereto.

(h) Wherever any constitutional provision or statute provides for, limits or measures the power or authority of any county, municipality or other taxing authority to levy taxes, borrow money or incur indebtedness in relation to the assessment of property therein for state taxes or for state and county taxes, such provision shall mean as assessed for county or municipal taxes, as the case may be.

(i) Except as otherwise provided in this Constitution, including any amendment thereto whenever adopted with respect to taxable property located in the city of Mountain Brook, the city of Vestavia Hills, or the city of Huntsville, the amount of ad valorem taxes payable to the state and to all counties, municipalities and other taxing authorities with respect to any item of taxable property described as Class I property shall never exceed 2 percent of the fair and reasonable market value of such taxable property in any one ad valorem tax year, such amount with respect to any item of Class II property shall never exceed 1½ percent of the fair and reasonable market value of such taxable property in any one ad valorem tax year, such amount with respect to any item of Class IV property shall never exceed 1¼ percent of the fair and reasonable market value of such taxable property in any one ad valorem tax year, and such amount with respect to any item of Class III property shall never exceed 1 percent of the fair and reasonable market value of such taxable property in any one ad valorem tax year. Whenever the total amount of ad valorem property taxes otherwise payable by any taxpayer with respect to any item of taxable property shall exceed in any one ad valorem tax year the maximum amount of such taxes permitted by this section, such amount of taxes shall be reduced by subtracting that amount of tax due that is in excess of the amount of tax otherwise permissible under the Constitution. In connection with the taxation of any item of taxable property, the amount of tax to be subtracted with respect to each authority levying and collecting any ad valorem property tax shall be in the same proportion to the total amount of tax to be subtracted that the total number of mills on each dollar of taxable property situated in the taxing authority levied by such taxing authority bears to the total number of mills on each dollar of taxable property situated in the taxing authority levied by all taxing authorities with respect to such item of taxable property. Before sending to any taxpayer any notice relating to the collection of ad valorem taxes, the tax collector in each county shall determine whether any portion of the amount of ad valorem property tax otherwise due with respect to any item of taxable property shall be subtracted pursuant to the provisions of this subsection and shall apportion the amount to be subtracted in accordance with the provisions of this subsection.

(j) Notwithstanding any other provision of this section, on and after October 1, 1978, taxable property defined in subsection (a) hereof as Class III property shall, upon application by the owner of such property, be assessed at the ratio of assessed value to the current use value of such taxable property and not the fair and reasonable market value of such property. The legislature may enact laws uniformly applicable to the state and all counties, municipalities and other taxing authorities establishing criteria and procedures for the determination of the current use value of any eligible taxable property and procedures for qualifying such property for assessment at its current use value. The legislature may also enact laws uniformly applicable to the state and all counties, municipalities and other taxing authorities providing for the ad valorem taxation of any taxable property ceasing to qualify for current use valuation; provided, however, that any additional tax on taxable property ceasing to qualify for current use valuation shall not apply to more than the three ad valorem tax years immediately preceding such cessation of qualification (including as one such year the year in which cessation of qualification occurs).

(k) The following property shall be exempt from all ad valorem taxation: the real and personal property of the state, counties and municipalities and property devoted exclusively to religious, educational or charitable purposes, household and kitchen furniture, all farm tractors, all farming implements when used exclusively in connection with agricultural property and all stocks of goods, wares and merchandise.

(l) Notwithstanding the other provisions of this section, with respect to the costs of reappraisal incident to the state-wide reappraisal of property heretofore authorized by the legislature, each county, municipality or other taxing authority for ad valorem tax years beginning on and after October 1, 1978, may impose and levy an additional ad valorem tax of not more than two mills on all taxable property located in the taxing authority in order to reimburse itself for its payment of such costs of reappraisal or to pay any unpaid costs or its pro rata share of such unpaid costs of reappraisal. The taxes provided for in this subsection, or any pro rata part thereof, shall terminate at the end of the ad valorem tax year in which sufficient funds are received from the taxes to pay in full the said reappraisal costs and any receipts from such taxes that are received during the ad valorem tax year of their termination that are not needed for the purposes specified herein may be used by the taxing authority levying the tax for general purposes of the taxing authority. The taxes authorized in this subsection shall not exceed in the aggregate, with respect to any item of taxable property located in the taxing authority, a total of two mills for all such taxes levied by all taxing authorities in a county and not two mills for each taxing authority in a county. If more than one such taxing authority in a county has paid or owes all or a portion of its reappraisal costs, such two mills shall be prorated among such taxing authorities in the county as they may agree, or if they cannot agree, in the percentage which each such taxing authority's costs of reappraisal bear to the total costs of reappraisal of all taxing authorities in the county. The provisions of this subsection shall apply only to the costs incurred by a taxing authority incident to the state-wide reappraisal of property heretofore authorized by the legislature, the amount of which costs shall be certified by the department of revenue, and shall not be applicable to any future reappraisals that may be required by law.

(m) If any portion of this section should be declared invalid by any court of competent jurisdiction, such invalidity shall not affect the validity of any of the remaining portions of this section, which shall continue effective.

Arkansas Constitution

Amend. No. 11. Art. XIV, §3. The General Assembly shall provide by the general laws for the support of common schools by taxes, which shall never exceed in any one year three mills on the dollar on the taxable property in the State. . . . Provided, that the General Assembly may, by general law, authorize school districts to levy by a vote of the qualified electors of such districts a tax not to exceed eighteen mills on the dollar in any one year for the maintenance of schools, the erection and equipment of school buildings. . . .

Provided, further, that no such tax shall be appropriated for any other purpose nor to any other district than that for which it is levied.

California Constitution

Art. XIII, §3.5. In any year in which the assessment ratio is changed, the Legislature shall adjust the valuation of assessable property described in subdivisions (o), (p) and (q) of Section 3 of this article to maintain the same proportionate values of such property.

Colorado Constitution

Art. V, §25. The general assembly shall not pass local or special laws in any of the following enumerated cases, that is to say: . . . remitting fines, penalties . . . granting to any corporation, association or individual any special or exclusive privilege, immunity or franchise, whatever. . . .

Art. XVIII, §7. **Land value increase—arboreal planting exempt.**—The general assembly may provide that the increase in the value of private lands caused by the planting of hedges, orchards and forests thereon, shall not, for a limited time to be fixed by law, be taken into account in assessing such lands for taxation.

Delaware Constitution

Art. VIII, §1. All taxes shall be uniform upon the same class of subjects within the territorial limits of the authority levying the tax, except as otherwise permitted herein, and shall be levied and collected under general laws passed by the General Assembly. County Councils of New Castle and Sussex Counties and the Levy Court of Kent County are hereby authorized to exempt from county taxation such property in their respective counties as in their opinion will best promote the public welfare. The county property tax exemption power created by this section shall be exclusive as to such property as is located within the respective counties. With respect to real property located within the boundaries of any incorporated municipality, the authority to exempt such property from municipal property tax shall be exercised by the respective incorporated municipality, when in the opinion of said municipality it will best promote the public welfare.

Florida Constitution

Art. III, § 11.
(a) There shall be no special law or general law of local application pertaining to:
. . . .
(2) assessment or collection of taxes for state or county purposes, including extension of time therefor. . . .
. . . .
(8) refund of money legally paid or remission of fines, penalties or forfeitures. . . .

Kentucky Constitution

§157. (Remove elipses in front of first sentence, page 56 of the first volume.)

§171. . . . .
Any law passed or enacted by the General Assembly pursuant to the provisions of or under this amendment, or amended section of the Constitution, classifying property and providing a lower rate of taxation on personal

property, tangible or intangible, than upon real estate shall be subject to the referendum power of the people, which is hereby declared to exist to apply only to this section, or amended section. The referendum may be demanded by the people against one or more items, sections, or parts of any act enacted pursuant to or under the power granted by this amendment, or amended section. . . .

§180. . . . Every act enacted by the General Assembly, and every ordinance and resolution passed by any county, city, town or municipal board or local legislative body, levying a tax, shall specify distinctly the purpose for which said tax is levied, and no tax levied and collected for one purpose shall ever be devoted to another purpose.

Louisiana Constitution

Art. VII, Pt. I, §2. [**Power to Tax; Limitation.**] The levy of a new tax, an increase in an existing tax, or a repeal of an existing tax exemption shall require the enactment of a law by two-thirds of the elected members of each house of the legislature.

Art. VII, Pt. II, §18.
(B) Classification. The classifications of property subject to ad valorem taxation and the percentage of fair market value applicable to each classification for the purpose of determining assessed valuation are as follows:

Classifications	Percentages
1. Land	10%
2. Improvements for residential purposes	10%
3. Electric cooperative properties, excluding land	15%
4. Public service properties, excluding land	25%
5. Other property	15%

The legislature may enact laws defining electric cooperative properties and public service properties.

Art. VII, Pt. II, §22. This Part shall not be applied in any manner which will (a) invalidate taxes authorized and imposed prior to the effective date of this constitution. . . .

Maryland Constitution

Art. III, §33. The General Assembly shall not pass local, or special Laws, in any of the following enumerated cases, viz.: For extending the time for the collection of taxes. . . .

Minnesota Constitution

Art. XII, §1. . . . The legislature shall pass no local or special law . . . remitting fines, penalties . . . exempting property from taxation . . . granting to any private corporation, association, or individual any special or exclusive privilege, immunity or franchise whatever or authorizing public taxation for a private purpose. . . .

Missouri Constitution

Art. III, §39. The general assembly shall not have power:
. . . .
(10) To impose a use or sales tax upon the use, purchase or acquisition of property paid for out of the funds of any county or other political subdivision.

Art. III, §40. The general assembly shall not pass any local or special law:
. . . .
(7) remitting fines, penalties. . . .

Nevada Constitution

Art. 4, §20. The legislature shall not pass local or special laws in any of the following enumerated cases—that is to say:
. . . .
For the assessment and collection of taxes for state, county, and township purposes. . . .

New Jersey Constitution

Art. IV, §VII, para. 9. The Legislature shall not pass any private, special or local laws:
. . . .
(6) Relating to taxation or exemption therefrom.
. . . .
(8) Granting to any corporation, association or individual any exclusive privilege, immunity or franchise whatever.
. . . .

New York Constitution

Art. III, §22. Every law which imposes, continues or revives a tax shall distinctly state the tax and the object to which it is to be applied, and it shall not be sufficient to refer to any other law to fix such tax or object. . . .

North Carolina Constitution

Art. II, §24. (1) The General Assembly shall not enact any local, private, or special act or resolution:

. . . .

(i) Remitting fines, penalties, and forfeitures, or refunding moneys legally paid into the public treasury;

. . . .

(k) Extending the time for the levy or collecion of taxes. . . .

. . . .

Ohio Constitution

Art. XII, § 5. **[Levying of taxes, and application.]**
No tax shall be levied, except in pursuance of law; and every law imposing a tax, shall state, distinctly, the object of the same, to which only, it shall be applied.

Pennsylvania Constitution

Art. VIII, §2(c). Citizens and residents of this Commonwealth, who served in any war or armed conflict in which the United States was engaged and were honorably discharged or released under honorable circumstances from active service, shall be exempt from the payment of all real property taxes upon the residence occupied by the said citizens and residents of this Commonwealth imposed by the Commonwealth of Pennsylvania or any of its political subdivisions if, as a result of military service, they are blind, paraplegic or double or quadruple amputees or have a service-connected disability declared by the United States Veterans' Administration or its successor to be a total or 100% permanent disability, and if the State Veterans' Commission determines that such persons are in need of the tax exemptions granted herein.

South Dakota Constitution

Art. II, § 23. The legislature is prohibited from enacting any private or special laws in the following cases:

. . . .

8. Remitting fines, penalties or forfeitures.

9. Granting to an individual association or corporation any special or exclusive privilege, immunity or franchise whatever.

. . . .

Art. XI, §8. No tax shall be levied except in pursuance of a law, which shall distinctly state the object of the same, to which the tax only shall be applied. . . .

Art. XI. (New Section). (Appendix B of the first volume, page 156: §13 is to be used.)

Texas Constitution

Art. VIII, §1. (No new paragraph after first sentence, Appendix B of the first volume, page 157.)

Art. VIII, §1-f. **Ad valorem tax relief.**—The legislature by law may provide for the preservation of cultural, historical, or natural history resources by:

(1) granting exemptions or other relief from state ad valorem taxes on appropriate property so designated in the manner prescribed by law; and

(2) authorizing political subdivisions to grant exemptions or other relief from ad valorem taxes on appropriate property so designated by the political subdivision in the manner prescribed by general law.

Art. VIII, § 3. **Taxes to Be Collected for Public Purposes Only.**—Taxes shall be levied and collected by general laws and for public purposes only.

Art. VIII, § 10. **Taxes Not to Be Released Except by Two-Thirds Vote of Each House.**—The Legislature shall have no power to release the inhabitants of, or property in, any county, city or town, from the payment of taxes levied for State or county purposes, unless in case of great public calamity in any such county, city or town, when such release may be made by a vote of two thirds of each house of the Legislature.

Utah Constitution

Art. VI, §28. The legislature shall not delegate to any special commission, private corporation or association, any power to make, supervise or interfere with any municipal improvement, money, property or effects, whether held in trust or otherwise, to levy taxes . . . or to perform any municipal functions.

Art. XIII, §10. All corporations or persons in this State, or doing business herein, shall be subject to taxation for State, County, School, Municipal or other purposes, on the real and personal property owned or used by them within the Territorial limits of the authority levying the tax.

Art. XIV, §8. The legislature by general law may authorize any county, city, or town to establish special districts within all or any part of the county, city, or town to be governed by the governing authority of the county, city, or town with power to provide water, sewerage, drainage, flood control, garbage, hospital, transportation, recreation, and fire protection services or any combination of these services and may authorize the county, city, or town: (1) to levy taxes upon the taxable property in only such districts for the purpose of acquiring, constructing, equipping, operating, and maintaining facilities required for any or all of these services . . . but the authority to levy taxes upon the taxable property in these districts . . . shall be conditioned upon the assent of a majority of the qualified electors of the district voting in an election for this purpose to be held as provided by law. Any such district created by a county may contain all or part of any incorporated municipality or municipalities but only with the consent of the governing authorities thereof. . . .

Virginia Constitution

Art. IV, §11. . . .
   No bill . . . which imposes, continues, or revives a tax, shall be passed except by the affirmative vote of a majority of all the members elected to each house. . . .
   Every law imposing, continuing, or reviving a tax shall specifically state such tax. . . .

Washington Constitution

Art. II, §28. The legislature is prohibited from enacting any private or special laws in the following cases:—
. . . .
   5. For assessment or collection of taxes, or for extending the time for collection thereof.
. . . .
   14. Remitting fines, penalties. . . .

Amend. 64. Art. VII, § 2.

. . . . Such aggregate limitation or any specific limitation imposed by law in conformity therewith may be exceeded only

(a) By any taxing district when specifically authorized so to do by a majority of at least three-fifths of the electors thereof voting on the proposition to levy such additional tax submitted not more than twelve months prior to the date on which the proposed levy is to be made and not oftener than twice in such twelve month period, either at a special election or at the regular election of such taxing district, at which election the number of persons voting "yes" on the proposition shall constitute three-fifths of a number equal to forty per centum of the total votes cast in such taxing district at the last preceding general election when the number of electors voting on the proposition does not exceed forty per centum of the total votes cast in such taxing district in the last preceding general election; or by a majority of at least three-fifths of the electors thereof voting on the proposition to levy when the number of electors voting on the proposition exceeds forty per centum of the total votes cast in such taxing district in the last preceding general election: PROVIDED, That notwithstanding any other provisions of this Constitution, any proposition pursuant to this subsection to levy additional tax for the support of the common schools may provide such support for a two year period;

. . . .

Amend. 58. Art. XI, §16.

. . . .

No legislative enactment which is a prohibition or restriction shall apply to the rights, powers and privileges of a city-county unless such prohibition or restriction shall apply equally to every other city, county, and city-county.

. . . .

. . . All taxes which are levied and collected within a municipal corporation for a specific purpose shall be expended within that municipal corporation.

The authority conferred on the city-county government shall not be restricted by the second sentence of Article 7, section 1* . . . of this Constitution.

Wyoming Constitution

Art. XV, § 6. **City levies limited.**—No incorporated city or town shall levy a tax to exceed eight mills on the dollar in any one year, except for the payment of its public debt and the interest thereon.

---

* Uniformity clause.

About the Author

Michael M. Bernard is a Fellow at the Lincoln Institute of Land Policy in Cambridge, Massachusetts, where he is doing work in law, taxation, and land-use controls. He received the A.B. degree from the University of Chicago and the J.D. from Northwestern University School of Law. After being admitted to the bar in Illinois and New York, he obtained a master's degree in planning from Harvard University. He has written, taught, and consulted in the areas of public-policy analysis and legal reform for a number of years. He served as a planning consultant and attorney-advisor in Puerto Rico, as planning and legal advisor to the city of Chicago, and as a consultant to Arthur D. Little, Inc., and the White House Policy Advisory Committee to the District Commissioners in an evaluation of District of Columbia area planning. During two successive administrations he was an advisor to the governor's office on the reorganization of Massachusetts state government, serving as the senior staff member responsible for setting up the Cabinet Office of Transportation and Construction.

Mr. Bernard was recently invited to be a member of the faculty of the American Law Institute on the subject of state constitutional constraints on the use of taxation as a land-use control.